THE DAILY PLANET

A HANDS-ON GUIDE TO A GREENER ENVIRONMENT

THE DAILY PLANET

A HANDS-ON GUIDE TO A GREENER ENVIRONMENT

PAUL GRISS

KEY PORTER BOOKS

Canadian Cataloguing in Publication Data

Griss, Paul

The daily planet

ISBN 1-55013-216-4

1. Environmental protection. 2. Commercial products – Environmental aspects. 3. Human ecology. I. Title.

TD170.2.G75 1990 304.2 C89-095260-4

Key Porter Books Limited
70 The Esplanade
Toronto, Ontario
Canada M5E 1R2

Design: Dreadnaught
Typesetting: Dreadnaught

Printed and bound in Canada
90 91 92 93 5 4 3 2 1

CONTENTS

To my parents

ACKNOWLEDGMENTS

The genesis of this book lies in the tremendous amount of attention paid to environmental issues in the latter part of the 1980s by the media. If one person can be credited with providing me with the inspiration, it was likely Peter Robb, who complained to me that people were becoming very aware of problems but very few solutions were being provided. It became apparent that many of the people who were being turned on to environmental issues perceived that the problems were "out there," and could be solved by cracking down on uncaring industries and governments. Recognition of the contribution of individuals to pollution and environmental degradation was not widespread.

This book benefited tremendously from the support of a number of people. Farley and Claire Mowat probably don't realize how important their simple comment that it was a "good idea" was at the time. Science Culture Canada came forward with a grant towards the research, and Paul Hackl did an excellent job of providing the background material. My thanks go out to Paul and to all those individuals and organizations who co-operated with him in his enquiries.

Shelley Bottomley helped with the difficult task of compiling and checking addresses and telephone numbers. Don Gamble and Diane Griffin have my deep appreciation for agreeing to review the manuscript and providing valuable commentary during extremely hectic periods in their lives. I would also like to acknowledge the members of the board of directors and staff of the Canadian Nature Federation for their support while I juggled the dual challenges of running the organization and producing a manuscript.

Most important of all, I'd like to thank my wife, Margaret, who, for several months, found me chained to my word processor for hours at a time. Her patience and support were essential as I tried to meet too many deadlines at once! And I can't forget Ginger, who entertained me and kept my feet warm.

INTRODUCTION

This we know: the Earth does not belong to man, man belongs to the 1
Earth. All things are connected like the blood that unites us all. Man did not weave the web of life, he is merely a strand in it. Whatever he does to the web, he does to himself.

Chief Seattle

The close of the twentieth century is a transitional period for the human race. In body we remain inalienably tied to the natural laws that govern all life on this planet. In mind, spurred by our rapidly advancing technology, we ignore those laws and act as though we are beyond such matters. As we become more urbanized and increasingly dependent on technology, our ties to nature weaken.

Finally, though, the Earth is reminding us of our place. Global warming, ozone depletion, acid rain, hazardous wastes, habitat loss, species extinction and other problems created or enhanced by humans have made us realize the environmental price of our success as a species. The impact of environmental degradation is every bit as devastating as a nuclear holocaust – and it is happening before our eyes. Yet, because the damage is mostly incremental, it is easier to ignore. A mushroom cloud conveys a strong threat to the safety of the individual. A dead fish does not.

In the face of these mammoth global problems, a sense of despair or fatalism is understandable. There are frequent calls to abandon our present values, ways and technology and return to a simpler existence. For most people, such a world is difficult to imagine; few have the courage to turn their backs on society and attempt such a lifestyle. For the rest of us, our challenge is to find ways to maintain and improve the quality of our lives, and those of people of other countries, while ensuring the protection of the environment that sustains us all. To do this, we must reconcile ourselves with nature and incorporate a concern for the natural environment into decision making at every level.

Certainly, the public seems willing to make changes. Opinion poll after opinion poll tells us that Canadians believe the state of the environment is one of the most important issues of our time, if not the most important. Considerable attention has been paid to alerting the public to what our smug approach to the natural environment has done to the planet on which we all depend, but less has been paid to demonstrating what can be done about it. This book offers concrete suggestions for action, both practical and political, and will, I hope, help you make informed choices.

The Role of the Individual

The disasters at Bhopal, Love Canal, Chernobyl, St. Basile le Grand and Valdez shocked the world. Yet every day, the individual actions of citizens and businesses worldwide may contribute far more to the degradation of the natural environment than any of these events did.

It is easy to believe that global environmental problems are the fault of governments or multinational corporations. In truth, though, each of us has far more responsibility for and influence over these issues than we perceive. Our desire for a high standard of living, and the resulting consumer demand, causes environmental destruction. Each and every one of us, through our daily activities, gives a stamp of approval to products or procedures that degrade the environment. We are all responsible for the present-day situation, and it is up to all of us, collectively, to chart a way out.

All of our daily personal decisions affect the environment. Whenever we use water or energy unnecessarily or buy something that has a huge environmental cost, we are encouraging waste or misuse of the scarce resources of this planet. Each individual contribution to the problem may be minimal, but the combined activities of our neighbours, our community and citizens across the country have an enormous effect.

Very few of our environmental problems are directly caused by wilful neglect on the part of greedy industries. The majority result from the unwitting actions and complacency of people just like you and me!

Some Basic Premises

In order to develop effective solutions and reduce our impact on the environment, we need to consider some basic facts that relate to all our environmental problems:

- **Humans are part of the natural environment**

The very fact that you are alive means that you are contributing to the despoliation of the environment. There are no innocents in this game. Just by providing for your basic needs of food, clothing and shelter you are affecting the world around you. Agricultural production, for example, denies other species the use of land and introduces massive amounts of chemicals into the environment. Most of us are, however, considerably removed from the activities necessary for survival, and it is easy for us to lose sight of the effects we have as individuals.

There are two extreme views of nature, which are both equally damaging. Subscribers to one see the natural world as something to exploit at all costs. Proponents of the other see nature as somehow separate from the human world, to be protected with minimal human interference. In both these views, humans are separate from the natural world; thus, both deny reality. We are an integral part of the natural environment. *Everything* we do affects the quality of that environment and, in turn, ultimately affects us.

- **Everything pollutes**

There is absolutely nothing that does not have an environmental cost in its production, its use or its disposal. When you breathe fresh air, you exhale carbon dioxide. When you drink fresh water, you urinate something totally different. There is, therefore, no point waiting for products to be developed that are completely safe; it won't happen. We *do* have a range of choices, though, and there is no excuse for using an environmentally harmful product when it is not necessary or when a less damaging alternative is available, even if the alternative costs more.

- **Everything dies**

As a society, we are obsessed with death. We take inordinate steps to prolong or preserve life, and we revere individuals who have survived for a long time, regardless of their contribution to society. Anything that even remotely threatens human health is opposed. Concerns over threats to health are important, but nothing is absolutely safe. All living things – humans included – die eventually. In the debate over environmental problems, however, we tend to become paranoid about anything that has even the slightest chance of causing health problems, while often ignoring more serious concerns.

More and more people are also opposing activities that result in the death of other forms of life by human hands, although they are often very selective about which life forms should be spared and which should not. Nobody is launching a crusade to save rats or mosquitoes, for example. Most judgments of "good" and "bad" applied to animals and plants are based on perception rather than reality. This further divorces us from the natural world.

Our survival depends on the death of other forms of life. Our food and most of the material we use for clothing and shelter come from living beings. Our use of land and water to provide for our needs denies many other species the use of that habitat, resulting in the death or displacement of animals and plants.

- **There are no easy answers**

If anyone tries to give you a rigid list of dos and don'ts respecting environmental protection, beware. There are no hard and fast solutions. All we can do is look for obvious signs of waste or misuse of resources. A perfect example is the concern over the use of chemicals called chlorofluorocarbons (CFCs) in plastic foam products (see Chapter 11). CFCs contribute to the destruction of the Earth's ozone layer, and concern over the issue has prompted a headlong rush to replace these chemicals. But consumers who think they are doing a good thing by purchasing "CFC-free" foam containers are ignoring the environmental costs of using plastic foam products in the first place.

▪ There are few villains

We all like to bash big business and government from time to time. However, we can't blame all our troubles on them. We are all responsible for the current state of affairs. We, as individuals, buy products from the very companies whose environmental performance we criticize. And we elect the politicians who, according to the public, don't do enough for the environment. If politicians and businesspeople have been ignoring the environment, it is because the public has allowed them to, and it is because *the public itself largely ignores the environment.* The individual who persists in driving an uneconomic vehicle that burns leaded gasoline, for instance, is as culpable as the corporation that resists pollution controls on its smokestack. The only difference is the scale.

Charting a Way Out of This Mess

Just as we cannot blame others for destroying the environment, so we cannot look to others to protect the environment. Responsibility for both begins at home. Changing our way of life to minimize our impact on the natural world and to use our resources more wisely will require a collective effort from the public and the corporate and government sectors. Political and business leaders are now at least *saying* the right things. We have to realize, though, that business and government follow us as much as we follow them. Politicians respond to public opinion, and business responds to the demands of its customers. If we, as consumers and voters, start demonstrating our concerns by taking steps as individuals to minimize our environmental impact, increased business and government activity will follow.

In addition, we can all help by getting involved beyond the home. Your first stop may be your workplace, where you and your co-workers can influence your employer's activities. If you own or run a business, you can start applying the same principles there that you do at home. You can also become a consumer activist.

You can also become more political. Many of the major environmental matters, such as waste disposal, fall under the jurisdiction of municipal governments. Getting involved in your community is one way of exerting your voting power and influencing government decision making. Your provincial or territorial government deals with broader environmental issues, primarily relating to natural resources. By lobbying at that level you can influence what is happening in your forests, for example. Finally, you can express your concerns at the federal level regarding environmental issues, such as energy policies, that are national or international in scope, or involve the activities of federal government departments or Crown corporations.

The higher the level of government, the less able an individual is to influence decisions. One way to improve your effectiveness is to support environmental groups that are already active at the municipal, provincial, national or international level. Some of the more reputable ones are listed in Appendix II. They need your moral and financial support to continue to operate effectively.

This book contains many suggestions for reducing your personal contribution to environmental destruction. It also provides questions that you can pose to governments and businesses to determine their approach to environmental matters. And, in some cases, it includes information on who to contact if you want to become more involved in specific issues.

Treating the Environment as if it Really Mattered

Aboriginal peoples the world over have an understanding of the natural world and their role in it. More than a century ago, Chief Seattle, whose words are quoted at the opening of this book, foretold the present-day situation: Our largely urbanized society has lost its connection with the natural world. Even when we do return to it, primarily for recreation, we do not achieve a great deal of intimacy with it. In fact, most people want to encounter nature only on their own terms!

Our eyes need to be opened soon if our society and the species with which we share this planet are to survive. It is not sufficient to place controls on smokestacks, or to eliminate lead in gasoline, or to avoid disposable plastic. We need to re-establish the connection with the natural world that should be integral to every one of us.

1

How to Be an Environmentally Conscious Consumer

Each of us, through our everyday purchasing decisions, contributes to the environmental problems that plague our world. Our challenge is to minimize our contribution as much as possible and to influence others to do the same. But since everything we do has an environmental cost, it is impossible to avoid doing any damage. The best we can do is to think through the implications of our purchasing decisions and daily actions. We each have to make our own judgments and consider the trade-offs we are willing to make.

It's Up to Us

We all want a comfortable standard of living. Products and services that once were unheard of, or luxuries, are today viewed as necessities. Other countries now also want to enjoy our standard of living. But, at the same time, people are waking up to the downside of this way of life and realizing that the world's resources simply cannot sustain the demands being placed upon them, let alone the pressures that will result as every country tries to attain North American levels of consumption.

It is not enough to enact environmental protection legislation; individual consumers have to make changes in their expectations and purchases if the pressures on the Earth's resources are to be reduced. Similarly, conservation measures, such as recycling, will not be fully effective if the demand for resources continues to grow. We can't keep using our raw materials to make products that are really not necessary or that we throw away.

We have to start applying the brakes. By becoming more environmentally aware and active, we can bring substantial pressure to bear on governments and industries to follow suit. If we reduce our demands, insist on products that are less damaging to the environment, and stop purchasing the ones that are most damaging, industries will fall all over themselves in an attempt to meet our new requirements. Otherwise, they will go out of business.

Re-assessing Our Needs

The initial step to becoming more environmentally conscious consumers is to question whether we really *need* many of the things we want or take for granted. We are under continual pressure to consume and are bombarded with advertisements promoting a plethora of products, most of which are not essential to the quality or enjoyment of life. And even if we are able to ignore these messages, we are still influenced by the purchasing patterns of our friends, relatives and neighbours.

The first mental leap that all of us must make is differentiating between what we really need and what others expect of us. This requires us to get rid of the "keeping up with the Joneses" attitude, which encourages people to overconsume. We fear that if we don't wear the right clothes, drive the right car and eat the right foods, others will assume we are badly off. Even worse, if we can obviously afford the "right things," but don't buy them, we run the risk of being labelled miserly or cheap.

There are some things we have always been led to believe are good, but they are not necessarily so. For example, the "beautiful" lawn and garden that our neighbours admire is often bought at great cost to the local environment. We can all make an immediate contribution to environmental protection simply by eliminating frivolous and wasteful products or actions from our lives. Do we really need to take the car to the corner store, water the lawn daily or stock a multitude of different household cleaners?

The Four Rs

To practise a more environmentally friendly lifestyle, you need only apply the three Rs: reduce, re-use and recycle. For industrial purposes, a fourth – recover – is added. In this book, we'll be adding our own fourth R – replace – since it provides options not included in the others. Adhering to these maxims will not only ease pressure on our natural environment, it will save you money! Let's look at them in order of importance and, conveniently, the ease with which they can be applied.

REDUCE

Question the need for everything you acquire or do, from buying a new car to driving it down the block. Conspicuous consumption, waste and the accumulation of material possessions place unnecessary pressures on natural resources and the environment. If we all learn to consume less, whether we can afford more or not, this pressure would be reduced. It would also be easier for other countries to attain our standard of living without a proportional increase in the demand on the world's resources.

REPLACE

When you do decide to buy or use a product, consider the alternatives. Take, for example, the use of cups for your office party. Your options include polystyrene containing CFCs (see Chapter 11), CFC-free foam, other plastic, paper, ceramic and glass. But the more fundamental question is the purpose to which the cups are put. If they can be re-used, then glass is preferable. You may be able to rent glass cups. If not, paper may be a more appropriate choice. When comparing products that are harmful to the environment – either in their manufacture or disposal – with ones that are more benign, always choose the latter even if they cost more.

RE-USE

Look for different uses for items in your possession or for ones that you would normally throw away. Lots of things can serve functions they weren't intended for. All you need is a little imagination. Remember, a jar is a jar is a jar! Whether your canister set is specially manufactured and imported or made from used jars, it's still a canister set. The only difference is in the perception.

In addition to finding new uses for products around your home, you can give unwanted possessions, such as books, to friends or neighbours, or to organizations that might make use of them.

RECYCLE

Many products such as glass bottles, paper, tin cans and some plastics can be recycled. Recycling is better than disposal, but it affects only a small portion of the goods in use and has little effect unless combined with the previous three principles.

Properly applied, these principles will help you to lessen your impact on the natural environment without lowering your standard of living.

Steps to Environmentally Conscious Shopping

There are very few clear choices between "good" and "bad" purchases. However, some are better or worse than others from an environmental perspective. Here are some basic rules to make your purchasing decisions easier. (Each of these will be referred to in greater detail throughout the following chapters.)

1 Buy only what you really need

Reducing consumption is the first step. We are all creatures of temptation. Each of our homes is full of junk that we were at one time convinced we needed. So are our landfill sites. We might as well throw our paper money directly into the garbage. It will take up less space, and it is biodegradable!

2 Buy quality

Buy the highest-quality item you can afford and have it repaired and serviced when necessary. Manufacturers still make high-quality, durable goods. Because these don't need to be replaced as often, they save money and resources in the long run.

Clothing is one area where this principle can be easily applied. Good-quality clothes and footwear can be tailored and mended to extend their lifespan. If we resist the temptation to buy the latest trend, our clothing requirements will be reduced considerably.

3 Buy for simplicity

Complexity is often confused with quality. The truth is that, generally, the more complex a product is, the more resources and energy have gone into its manufacture. Unless the bells and whistles are absolutely essential to your intended use of the product, select the simpler model.

The same principle applies to processing. The more refined or processed a product, the more resources required in its production. Most processed foods, particularly items like single-serving dinners, are not only costly to produce (hence their high price), but also overpackaged. Purchase products that undergo as little processing as possible.

4 Buy for energy efficiency

When purchasing a product that consumes energy, whether it is driven by electricity or petroleum products, select the one that is most energy-efficient. Often, the initial cost may be higher (though in the case of cars the inverse is usually true); however, the reduced operating costs should allow you to recoup the increased initial outlay over time.

5 Avoid disposable products

Very few things that are sold as disposable actually are. Sure, they can be thrown away; anything can. But in most cases they don't go away. Their useful life may be over, but, unless they can be recycled or are composed of materials that will degrade, they will be around for a long time. It is a terrible waste of resources to produce things that will end up in the garbage after only one or two uses. Perhaps one of the most ludicrous examples is the disposable camera.

6 Buy locally

Transportation costs should be a factor in your purchasing decisions. If two items of comparable quality are available, buy the one that was produced closest to your own home. Not only will you be supporting your friends and neighbours, you will be rejecting the unnecessary transport of goods. If perfectly good lettuce is produced in your region, why should energy be expended to transport it from California?

7 Buy in bulk

When buying food, or other products to be consumed in quantity, buy the largest amount that you can easily store and use. Not only will you reduce the amount of packaging you purchase, you will also find it cheaper and you'll expend less energy on repeated trips to the store.

8 Avoid packaging

Packaging, particularly of food products and cosmetics, is one of the worst environmental offenders, since it is a major component of garbage and is largely unnecessary. Some types of packaging are totally inappropriate for the product, such as single servings of food in hard plastic containers. For the sake of a few mouthfuls, a package that takes up a large amount of space and will remain with us for decades is employed. Some packaged products, such as the individually wrapped baked potato, are downright silly. (For a few guidelines to help you assess packaging, see Chapter 12.)

9 Buy recycled products

When possible, buy products that are made from recycled material. Only if markets develop for these goods will recycling programs be successful. This concept also applies to buying goods second-hand, particularly in cases where quality is not important. Outfitting a child in state-of-the-art equipment to try a sport for the first time is a waste if the child quickly loses interest in the sport.

10 Favour products that are less costly to the environment

If you buy goods and services that cause less environmental damage than their competitors (like unbleached paper products), you will encourage manufacturers and other businesses to make and market more of these products. If alternatives are not available, then don't buy unless you absolutely have to. Goods and services that no one wants aren't around for long.

11 Carry your own bags Most stores offer you a bag no matter how small your purchase. Going from store to store within a mall, you can easily end up with bags within bags within bags! Then, when you get home, you have to figure out what to do with all of them. The answer is simple. Take your own bag when you shop – either a good-quality canvas bag, or a plastic bag that you were given on a previous trip. As long as you hang on to the receipts for the things you purchase, you shouldn't encounter trouble.

12 Share major items It's amazing how the domino effect works in a neighbourhood. As soon as Joe buys a snowblower, they start cropping up everywhere. Virtually every house on most streets has a lawnmower, and many will have snowblowers and a variety of other equipment and tools. Most of these will be used only sporadically. If you live in a relatively stable neighbourhood, you might consider pooling resources, or paying one of the neighbourhood kids to cut your lawn or to shovel your drive.

13 Rent instead of buying Many of the things that you need only occasionally, such as tools, Rototillers or party supplies, can be rented or borrowed. Why spend your money and use resources to buy something that will sit unused or, worse, be thrown away?

14 Be prepared to pay more in the short term Improving the environmental performance of businesses takes an influx of capital. The costs involved, like all business costs, are passed on to the consumer. Understandably, when pricing is competitive, many industries and businesses are loath to be the first to spend money on things like better waste treatment, because it will make their products more expensive than those of their competitors. Although consumers say they will pay more for products that are less harmful to the environment, industries are going to need some concrete assurance before taking a substantial risk.

15 Make sure money talks the right language

Destroying the environment is not a privilege that can be bought. Paying a lot of money for a wasteful or unneeded product or activity only reinforces the market for that product or service. Products that are more environmentally friendly than others are likely to cost more in the short term, but investing in them is a far wiser application of your money.

16 Beware the come-on

It didn't take marketers long to notice the public's interest in environmental protection and to claim that their products or services are better for the environment than their competitors'. The maxim "buyer beware" still applies. A good example is "environmentally-friendly" gasoline. Look beyond the claims to assess for yourself whether the product or service lives up to its billing.

17 Be a critic

If you buy a product or service that is less damaging to the environment than its competitors, write to the competitors to tell them why you are favouring someone else's product. If you avoid a product or service because of its environmental impact, write and urge the company to develop a more environmentally sensitive approach. A well-reasoned argument can carry a lot of weight. Sponsors have pulled their advertisements from television shows on the basis of a single letter of complaint. If a business believes that public concern is affecting its balance sheet, it will listen.

18 A little hypocrisy is okay

Total austerity is impossible to achieve. A friend of mine is a vegetarian, yet he eats eggs. I rib him about it, but he understands the hypocrisy and accepts it. He feels he is causing much less animal suffering than if he were not a vegetarian in the first place. If similar small compromises are the price of progress on environmental matters, then so be it.

Starting Down the Path

As the saying goes, the longest journey starts with a single step. In the face of monumental problems, it is easy to be fatalistic and feel that we can't make a difference. But if we learn to think of how all of our actions affect the environment, and if each of us makes a few changes, before long we'll be well down the path toward a better relationship with our planet. Throughout this book, you will find recommendations and directions to help you on your way. We all want to make a difference. Let's look at some ways – big and small – in which we can each help.

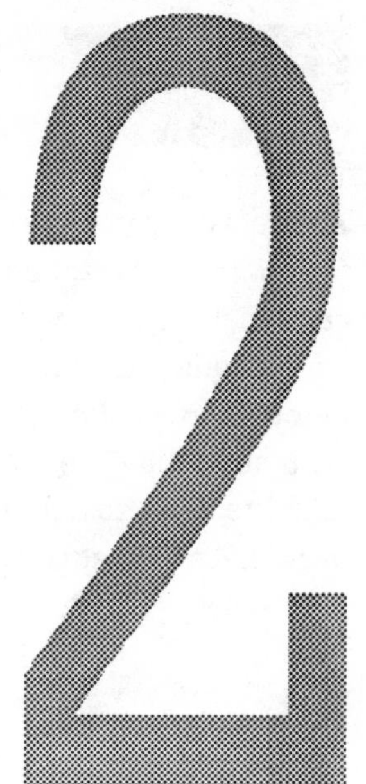

Fuelling the Fires

In March 1989, the oil tanker Exxon Valdez hit a reef shortly after sailing from the port of Valdez, Alaska. More than forty million litres of crude oil were spilled into the pristine waters of Prince William Sound, killing untold numbers of birds, marine mammals and aquatic life. Although most observers knew that a spill of such magnitude was inevitable in those waters, howls of public protest erupted over the culpability of the tanker's crew and company officials.

Incidents like the Exxon Valdez spill graphically illustrate the environmental risks posed by our thirst for energy. But it is all too easy to distance ourselves from responsibility for such environmental problems. Ultimately, however, we are to blame. It is our demand for energy that contributes significantly to global warming, to the likelihood of oil spills, to the possibility of nuclear accidents and to other documented problems. Yet energy consumption continues to increase. *Canadians are the highest users of energy per capita in the world.*

Global Warming

The glass in greenhouses allows the rays of the sun to enter but prevents the heat from dissipating. Consequently, the temperature inside the greenhouse is elevated without the use of other forms of energy. Plants can thus be grown indoors out of season at little cost. Our atmosphere works in a similar fashion. As the Earth absorbs the sun's rays, gases (primarily carbon dioxide) and particles in the atmosphere prevent heat from being easily dissipated back into space. This is the so-called "greenhouse effect." As a result, the Earth retains heat, which is necessary for life to exist. However, a build-up of "greenhouse" gases and particles is believed to be intensifying the greenhouse effect, causing warming of the atmosphere and changing weather patterns. Some people would no doubt welcome warmer weather, but the implications of global warming could be far more dramatic than that.

Warmer weather in the north could result in a melting of polar ice caps, a rise in the level of the world's oceans and a flooding of low-lying areas. Precipitation patterns could also change, which would wreak havoc on agriculture and reforestation as growing seasons are altered. The distribution of wildlife could be changed, and the present boundaries of protected areas might no longer be appropriate.

▪ **Fossil fuels** are the human species' main contribution to the problem. Every time coal, oil and natural gas are burned, they release carbon and other pollutants into the atmosphere. Left alone, nature copes with the increased carbon levels from natural sources. Some is absorbed by the ocean and some is recruited for photosynthesis in plants. But natural systems cannot deal with the incredible amount of carbon that humans are introducing into the atmosphere through the burning of fossil fuels.

▪ **Methane** is produced when organic material breaks down naturally. It can be released through biological decay in areas such as marshes, bogs, swamps and rice paddies. One of the major sources of methane is from the digestive systems of ruminants, especially cattle. Cow flatulence, believe it or not, is a major contributor to global warming, as is decomposing cow manure.

▪ **Fire** burns trees and plants, releasing carbon into the atmosphere and producing smoke, which enhances the greenhouse effect. Forest fires, the use of wood as fuel, and the burning of crops all contribute to global warming.

▪ **Deforestation** reduces the amount of living plant matter. Plants use carbon dioxide in the process of photosynthesis and therefore help to remove carbon from the atmosphere. Every tree cut reduces the Earth's ability to respond to carbon build-up.

How Much Fossil Fuel Do Canadians Use?

	1988	1978
Petroleum	262,200 m³/day	289,900 m³/day
Natural Gas	183 million m³/day	144 million m³/day
Coal	54,382 kilotonnes/yr	31,737 kilotonnes/yr

- Canadians' demand for petroleum declined to 236,200 m³/day by 1983 but has been increasing since.
- In 1988, the daily demand for petroleum products included 93,300 m³ of gasoline, 45,600 m³ of diesel fuel, 37,100 m³ of ethane, propane and butane, 24,500 m³ of heavy fuel oil, 18,200 m³ of light fuel oil and 13,800 m³ of aviation fuel.

(Source: Energy, Mines and Resources Canada)

Canadian Electricity Production

	1988	1978
Hydroelectricity	303,546 GW.H (62%)	234,039 GW.H (70%)
Thermal (Coal burning)	107,324 GW.H (22%)	72,171 GW.H (21%)
Nuclear	78,176 GW.H (16%)	29,435 GW.H (9%)
TOTAL	489,046 GW.H	335,645 GW.H

Note: GW.H = gigawatt.hours (giga = billion)

- In 1966, hydroelectricity accounted for 82% of total electricity production in Canada but is declining in proportion as the use of coal and nuclear energy grows.
- The increased Canadian demand for coal between 1978 and 1988 (see previous table) is almost entirely due to greater production of thermal electricity. Use of coal for that purpose doubled from 22,914 kilotonnes in 1978 to 45,970 kilotonnes in 1988. Use of coal for steel production declined from 6,909 kilotonnes in 1978 to 6,261 kilotonnes in 1988.

(Sources: Energy, Mines and Resources Canada; Environment Canada)

Canadian Energy Sources

Canada benefits from a wide variety of energy sources, which gives us a lot of latitude in selecting our fuels. Depending on the region, we can choose from oil, natural gas, coal, wood, hydroelectricity and nuclear power. Each of these sources of energy has its advantages and disadvantages, and none of them is without environmental cost.

Fossil Fuels

The vast majority of energy used worldwide is derived from the burning of carbon-based products – coal, oil and natural gas – commonly referred to as fossil fuels. The extraction, refining and transportation of these fuels are huge undertakings, requiring significant amounts of energy themselves and causing much damage to the environment. The burning of fossil fuels for industry, transportation and home heating, among other uses, is the major contributor to global air pollution and one of the primary causes of the trend toward warming of the Earth's atmosphere.

Oil, or petroleum, is the predominant energy source in Canada, although other sources are gaining. Almost 40% of all the energy produced in Canada is in this form, and about 18% of Canadian homes are heated by oil. When refined, petroleum produces heating oil, gasoline, diesel fuel, propane, butane, lubricating oils and a wide variety of other products. Generally, the more refined the product, the cleaner it will burn. However, the refining process itself uses a great deal of energy and produces pollution.

The use of natural gas is growing; approximately 30% of energy in Canada is produced by this fuel. It is the major fuel for home heating, supplying 45% of our homes. The cleanest of the fossil fuels, natural gas is plentiful. It is expected to become a much more important source of energy in the coming years. Natural gas is most efficiently transported by pipelines, which cross thousands of kilometres of land, disrupting wildlife and the environment. In 1982, Canada had 169,000 kilometres of natural gas pipelines, an increase of 220% since 1960.

One of the major problems with oil and natural gas is that supplies are located a long way from markets, frequently in environmentally sensitive areas. Therefore, the extraction and transportation of these fuels poses a number of environmental risks.

Worldwide coal consumption is also increasing, which is particularly surprising since coal has been recognized for centuries as a dirty fuel. Coal produces approximately 15% of Canadian energy, up substantially in recent years but still well below the world average of approximately 30%. As with oil and natural gas, environmental problems result not only from burning coal but also from its extraction (see Chapter 5).

All coal is not alike; each type has its own properties, with harder coal generally burning more cleanly. In Canada, three types – bituminous (32% in 1988), subbituminous (43%) and lignite (25%) – are used most. Bituminous coal once predominated in Canada because of its high energy content, but subbituminous coal is now preferred. Although it produces less energy than bituminous coal, subbituminous coal also contains less sulphur and thus contributes less to the acid rain problem (see Chapter 3).

Electricity

Electricity heats about 32% of Canadian homes and powers most of our appliances and lights. The majority of electricity in Canada is generated by harnessing rivers to produce hydroelectricity. In recent years, however, the use of coal and nuclear power to generate electricity has been growing. None of these energy sources is risk- or damage-free: burning coal contributes to atmospheric pollution; hydroelectric developments flood wildlife habitat; nuclear power presents an unacceptable risk and creates hazardous wastes that must be safely stored.

Despite Canada's wealth of water, our hydroelectric potential is not unlimited. It is estimated that more than half Canada's available capacity is now being exploited, and this output accounts for about 10% of Canada's energy production. The major beneficiary of the development of the remaining potential will be the United States, whose demand for Canadian hydroelectricity is expected to increase by 50% in the next ten years. Unlike other sources of power, however, the major environmental costs of hydroelectricity do not relate to its use but to the reservoirs and transmission lines necessary to its generation.

To form reservoirs, huge amounts of land are flooded, destroying wildlife habitat, killing or displacing wildlife, harming water quality and causing permanent damage to the environment of the region (see Chapter 6). Hydroelectric projects also require the construction of hundreds of kilometres of transmission lines, which cut straight through the lands between the dam and the beneficiary of the power, again affecting wildlife habitat. In 1982, Canada had a total of 184,271 km of electrical transmission lines, up 80% from 1960.

Canada presently has six operating nuclear power stations, in Ontario, Quebec and New Brunswick, with a total of nineteen reactors on line. Ontario has made the major nuclear commitment to date in Canada, with slightly less than half its thermally generated electricity derived from nuclear sources. About 3% of Canada's total energy production is from nuclear sources.

No source of power is as controversial as nuclear energy. The nuclear industry has seized upon the current concern about global warming and other environmental problems caused by the burning of carbon-based fuels as ammunition to promote nuclear energy. Yet there are also reasons to challenge the industry's claim that nuclear power is clean, safe and the solution to our energy problems. Although nuclear accidents are rare, their effects can be catastrophic and far-reaching. Mining uranium, which provides the fuel for nuclear reactors, has serious environmental consequences (see Chapter 5). Used fuel from nuclear reactors remains highly radioactive for centuries, presenting problems for safe storage.

We must, of course, move away from traditional fuels eventually. Turning to nuclear energy, however, will simply exchange one set of problems for another. Other countries recognize the danger. No new nuclear reactors have been ordered in the United States, for example, since 1978.

Other Sources of Energy

Fossil fuels, hydroelectricity and nuclear power account for all but a small amount of the energy consumed by Canadians. The balance comes from a wide variety of sources, mostly experimental. Although all our present sources of energy are known to have environmental drawbacks, little effort is being made to explore alternatives, despite the fact that, as the world runs out of fossil fuels and uranium, and as it uses up its hydroelectric potential, we'll have little choice but to switch.

Batteries are the most common of the other forms of energy we encounter. They are a mobile and "disposable" source of electricity, which they produce by chemical energy. You won't hurt the environment by *using* them, but their *disposal* poses many problems. Like other disposable products, throwing them away after their short useful life wastes all the resources used in their manufacture. Depending on the type, batteries contain a variety of highly corrosive materials and toxic chemicals including mercury, cadmium and lead. In a landfill site, the casing of the battery corrodes and the chemicals can then leak into the environment. Eventually, they may find their way into a water supply. Rechargeable batteries and recycling of used batteries could reduce these problems.

Other alternate sources of power include burning hydrogen, generation of electricity from wind and tides, harnessing the sun's rays, creation of biologically based fuels from plants, and deriving energy from waste. Research into these new types of energy is not as aggressive as it should be, but if energy prices rise and supplies are short, attention to alternatives will grow.

There may already be some non-traditional energy sources around your home; solar-powered calculators, watches and other small appliances are becoming more widely available. Home heating can also be augmented by the use of solar-powered water heaters and heating systems. Ground energy systems pump heat from the earth, which fluctuates very little in temperature seasonally, to warm homes. Entrepreneurs are continually developing new options for the consumer who wants to explore alternatives.

▪ ***What is the source of your household energy supply?***
Do you have an oil or natural gas furnace? Does your local utility produce electricity from hydro power or nuclear energy, or does it burn coal? If coal, what sort of coal does it burn and what is the rationale for doing so? What plans are in place to control or reduce the pollution produced by thermal electricity generation or to switch to cleaner fuels? Is your community looking at alternative sources of power?

▪ ***Support energy alternatives***
Contact Energy, Mines and

Resources Canada and your provincial ministry of energy to find out what governments are doing to explore alternate forms of energy supply. Ask politicians why they continue to subsidize use of polluting sources of energy while reducing commitments to research into new sources. Visit home shows and other events where promoters of alternate power sources may display their wares.

Energy Hot Spots

Oil and Gas Development

As demand for oil and gas increases, industry must look farther and farther afield for new reserves. From an environmental perspective, the risks of exploration and development are growing. Most new development will occur either offshore or in sensitive arctic environments. The establishment of industrial activity in such areas, and the associated traffic, affects wildlife and the environment. The greatest threat is from accidents, whether at the drilling site or during transport of the oil or gas by tanker or pipeline.

If the Exxon Valdez spill and the other major and minor spills have proven one thing, it is that the oil industry is unable to respond quickly and effectively to spills even when they are in relative proximity to major ports or centres of human population. Should such an accident occur in sensitive arctic environments, the effects on wildlife and the environment would be catastrophic and could last for decades, or even longer. It's a safe bet that northern communities and review boards, in the wake of the Exxon Valdez spill, are going to insist on stringent environmental controls on new developments in their regions.

Potential areas of conflict include the Beaufort Sea, Lancaster Sound, Hibernia (off Newfoundland), and oil exploration off the west coast of British Columbia. One of the more controversial projects involves the construction of a natural gas pipeline down the Mackenzie Valley. Although this idea was shelved in 1978, it has resurfaced. Several energy companies are applying for permission to export natural gas from the Beaufort Sea to the United States. Although no formal proposal has been made to date, the preferred form of transportation would be a Mackenzie Valley pipeline.

CONTACT: Canadian Arctic Resources Committee
Canadian Nature Federation

Hydroelectricity Exports

Export deals are being negotiated around the country by major producers of hydroelectric power. Often, buyers are guaranteed a steady supply of electricity for a relatively low price; the long-term environmental costs of dams are rarely considered. The Quebec government is aggressively pursuing the development of its remaining hydroelectric potential. Virtually all this new power, which would come from the second phase of the James Bay project and the damming of rivers along the north shore of the Gulf of St. Lawrence, would be exported to the northeastern United States.

The James Bay I hydroelectric project in northern Quebec flooded an area of land the size of Jamaica. Although they profited financially from the project, many natives of the region are determined to oppose the next phase of construction. They don't want a repeat of James Bay I's unforeseen effects on the land and their lifestyle. The U.S.-based National Audubon Society has already begun to campaign against James Bay II. They are concerned about the damage that it will do to James Bay, which is extremely important to migratory waterfowl.

CONTACT: National Audubon Society
Canadian Nature Federation

Investment in Energy Conservation

In the last few years, the federal government has adopted a prominent international stance on environmental protection, particularly atmospheric pollution. Yet, at the same time, it is spending millions of dollars to subsidize new oil and gas developments and has slashed budgets for federal programs to promote energy conservation. This hypocrisy sends mixed messages to Canadians and is one of the major barriers to real progress on the energy front.

CONTACT: Energy Probe
Friends of the Earth

Energy Conservation

Finding a plentiful source of energy that won't hurt the environment, that isn't risky to generate or transport, and that people will accept and use is a monumental challenge. In the meantime, the best option open to us is to conserve energy. At present, *energy conservation is the cheapest and safest source of new energy supplies.* If everyone used less, more would be available to satisfy new demand. Conservation saves the consumer money and reduces pollution.

Energy consumption in Canada is actually increasing, even with the current public concerns about global warming. More than one-third of Canada's energy is consumed by industry. Approximately the same amount goes to residential, commercial and agricultural uses. The balance is used for transportation.

You can influence all three areas. By selecting products that require minimal application of energy in their production, you can help to encourage energy conservation on the part of industry. Ways to do this are discussed throughout this book. As a general rule, the more processing an item has undergone, the more energy is likely to have been used in its manufacture.

Transportation itself is covered directly in the next chapter. However, transportation is also an indirect factor in most products you use every day, since most goods purchased must be transported to market. By purchasing products that are produced locally, you can save energy in the transportation sector.

The most direct contribution that each of us can make, though, is to conserve energy in our own homes. Roughly one-third of your household energy consumption will be for heating or cooling your home. The remainder is about equally divided between your water heater and your appliances, with lighting accounting for a small portion. By saving energy in these areas, you'll reduce pressures on our environment and save money as well.

Home Heating and Cooling

Our climate is one of the major reasons that Canadians are the highest per capita consumers of energy in the world. Few of us would put up with an unheated home or office, and, for many, a house or office that is not air-conditioned is unthinkable. But a little moderation is possible. Many Canadian homes and offices are overheated and overcooled.

There are a number of ways you can minimize the energy used to heat and cool your home. The method of construction and layout of your home contribute to the home's energy requirements, but your lifestyle can also affect energy consumption.

HOW TO SAVE ENERGY IN HEATING AND COOLING YOUR HOME

1 **Choose a home design that permits selective heating** Open-concept homes are aesthetically pleasing but require a lot of energy to keep comfortable. Houses with a lot of rooms and doors allow you to heat only those areas you need to. Turn down heat, or close heating registers, in rooms that are not in use.

2 **Use the cleanest energy supply possible** Your options in home heating will depend on where you live. Generally, electricity, as it is centrally produced, is better, with hydroelectricity having the least environmental cost in its use. Natural gas is preferable to oil for heating. If you have an oil furnace, consider changing it to gas.

3 **Upgrade your furnace** Newer furnaces are more efficient. Compare the performance of your furnace with that of others available. You may find that over the long term an upgrade will save you money.

4 **Examine ways to supplement your home heating system** Talk to suppliers of solar or ground energy systems. Depending on where you live and your energy requirements, these options, as well as other less conventional choices, may save you energy and money.

5 **Avoid "cosmetic" heat** Wood stoves and fireplaces are attractive additions to homes. However, unless they are properly installed and operated, most of the heat they generate simply goes out the chimney, wasting wood (or coal) and money.

6 Don't let the outside in

Few houses these days have lobbies or porches. However, both can help to reduce the heat you lose every time you open the door. Storm doors and windows also help. Weatherstrip around doors to reduce drafts. Caulk cracks around door and window frames. (Note: Don't go overboard. A home that is sealed too tightly is not good for you as fresh air is essential to health.)

7 Upgrade your insulation

Insulation is particularly important in older homes. Material now available has much better insulative properties than that in use only a few years ago. Some forms of insulation also settle or compact over time, reducing their effectiveness. Heat is also lost through windows. Windows with good insulative properties are available, and you might consider replacing your windows with ones that are more energy-efficient.

8 Have your home's efficiency audited

Contact your local utility, or provincial energy ministry, to ask if they have an "energy audit" program. If they do, you should be able to arrange an inspection of your home to help you identify areas where energy efficiency can be improved.

9 Take advantage of free energy

Use sunshine to heat your house. Open curtains and blinds in the cooler months. (In summertime, close them to keep temperatures down.) Energy produced by heat-generating appliances like ovens and clothes dryers can also supplement your home heating system in winter. Avoid using these appliances during the warmer parts of summer days to help keep your house cool.

10 Turn the heat down

Set the room temperature in rooms you use at 20 degrees Celsius. Wear a sweater or use a space heater if you find it cool. Turn down the heat still farther at night and when the house is unoccupied.

11 Turn down your water heater

In order to have hot water ready when we need it, we keep our hot water heaters full at all times. For most applications, the hot water that comes out of the tap is blended with cold to reduce its temperature. Why heat it so hot in the first place? Dropping the temperature of your hot water heater will save energy. Insulating hot water pipes will also reduce the amount of energy wasted as the water cools between the tank and the tap.

Appliances and Their Use

There has been a proliferation of small appliances in North America in the past few decades. New devices gain widespread acceptance if they provide entertainment or can be shown to save our most prized commodity – time. How many people had heard of microwave ovens or videocassette recorders ten years ago? Now they are staples in many Canadian homes. Using these appliances requires electricity and, of course, the raw materials necessary to construct the appliance in the first place.

In 1988, 478,000 washing machines and 413,000 clothes dryers were sold in Canada. Canadians also bought 522,000 refrigerators, 260,000 freezers, 507,000 ranges and 309,000 dishwashers that year. Sales have been growing steadily for several years. Sales of dishwashers, for example, increased by 70% over 1984. In addition to these major appliances, households contain a wide variety of other equipment, such as televisions and stereos, as well as a plethora of small electrical devices from mixers to power tools.

Each appliance places different demands on your household energy supply. Those that produce heat, such as ranges and clothes dryers, use the most energy. The amount of energy required to run an appliance is indicated by its wattage. Utilities charge for electricity by the kilowatt hour; your utility bill therefore measures how long you use an appliance as well as its wattage. Running something of low wattage continuously can use as much electricity and cost as much as occasionally using something of high wattage. Therefore, while your refrigerator requires far less power than your stove, it will likely account for a greater portion of your electricity bill because it operates constantly.

Reducing Appliance Energy Consumption

1 Question the need
Appliances make life easier, and many have become so much a part of our routine that we cannot imagine life without them. But next time you reach to turn on an appliance, ask whether its use is necessary.

2 Look for alternatives
Try drying clothes on a clothesline. If you do this inside during the winter, you will also minimize the need for a humidifier. Dry your hair with a towel. Mix food ingredients by hand. Pick an activity like sawing wood or cutting grass and do it manually. Look for alternate forms of entertainment to those provided by televisions, stereos and battery-powered toys and games. For virtually every appliance, alternatives that save energy or provide exercise are available.

3 Select for energy efficiency
Most major manufacturers now produce appliances that are designed to be energy efficient. The initial costs of these appliances may be higher, but they will be cheaper to operate over the long term. Buy the most efficient one available.

4 Use the right appliance
Your electric stove requires more electricity than any other appliance. A broiler or microwave oven consumes far less energy. Use them especially for small meals or single servings. When cooking on top of your stove, choose the element or burner that best fits the size of pan in use.

5 Use cleaner energy sources
Electrically powered appliances are preferable to those that run on gasoline. When buying or renting (or borrowing) a lawnmower, weed trimmer or snowblower, for example, choose the electrically powered model.

6 Use your major appliances efficiently
Do fewer loads of laundry and don't use the washing machine unless you have a full load. Detergent manufacturers tell you to separate your laundry because they want you to use more detergent. Use a dishwasher only when you have a full load. Wash smaller numbers of dishes in the sink.

7 Compensate for the inefficiencies of your appliances
If your freezer is not full, fill the empty space with newspapers. The dissipation of heat from large appliances, such as a range, can help to heat your home. Opening your dishwasher before the dry cycle starts can humidify your home as the dishes dry naturally.

8 Don't use more light than you need
Select the wattage of light bulbs according to the requirements of the area – 40- or 60-watt bulbs for normal use and 100 watts for reading. If your light fixture requires several bulbs, remove one or two rather than burn energy unnecessarily.

9 Use energy-efficient light
Fluorescent and mercury vapour bulbs have higher installation costs but use far less energy and last much longer than regular light bulbs. Compact fluorescent bulbs can replace incandescent bulbs for most uses.

10 Turn appliances off
If no one is watching the television or listening to the radio, turn it off. Similarly, why leave lights burning if nobody is in the room? If you want lights on for security while you are out, place them on a timer.

11 Avoid disposable power
When using battery-operated appliances and gadgets, use rechargeable batteries where possible. Many municipalities include batteries in their household hazardous waste disposal programs, and used batteries can be recycled.

12 Reduce barbeque pollution
Charcoal briquets and lighter fluid are dirty fuels that release pollutants and carbon dioxide. Use of a gas barbeque is preferable.

Energy Conservation Is Integral to Environmental Protection

Energy is a constant theme throughout this book because everything we do requires energy, and its use is without a doubt the pre-eminent contributor to the environmental problems facing the world today. The next several decades must see the development of clean technologies to meet the world's energy requirements. But until better sources of energy are available, we have little option but to minimize the amount of energy we use individually and as a society. We can all make a major impact in this area by controlling our own personal use of energy and by choosing products and services that are energy efficient.

3

The Costs of Getting Around

Without a doubt, the most damaging thing that most Canadians do to the environment is drive a car. And yet, many of us view cars and the freedom that they represent as a right and a necessity. Despite the pollution problems and restricted supply of fossil fuels, analysts predict that in coming years the number of cars on the roads will escalate, average speeds will decline and the number of annual traffic fatalities will double.

Most Canadian cities have been modified to cater to the automobile. Neighbourhoods are destroyed to build freeways, suburbs sprawl to accommodate cars and green space is paved over for roads and parking space. Virtually any major city can provide examples of the absurdity that automobile travel has become. Freeways with 100 km/h speed limits and many lanes proceed at a crawl solely because of the volume of traffic attempting to use them. Yet people continue to buy cars and to drive inefficiently.

Air travel also shows no signs of slowing down. Congestion in the skies in some areas is as great a problem as it is on the ground. At one time trains and buses were preferred forms of transportation. Now people avoid them in favour of cars and airplanes, except in heavily populated areas where they are almost essential for many people. Governments contribute to the problem by insisting that travellers pay as much of the costs of trains and buses as possible, while simultaneously using the non-driving taxpayers' money to maintain roads for automobiles, thereby giving drivers a price advantage.

Transportation Facts

• In 1987, 15.9 million road vehicles were registered in Canada, including 11.8 million automobiles, 3.5 million trucks, 414,000 motorcycles and 59,000 buses.

• Since 1984, Canadian drivers have purchased, on average, more than 1 million new cars each year.

• The number of two-car families grew by almost 400,000 from 1977 to 1981.

• Canadians consumed 93,300,000 litres of gasoline each day in 1988.

• There were roughly 240,400 kilometres of paved roads in Canada in 1975, an increase of 112% since 1960.

• In 1975, Canada had approximately 66,400 kilometres of railroad tracks, down 7% from 1960.

• In 1986, approximately 23 million passengers rode on Canada's trains, for a total of 2,831 million kilometres.

• In 1985, 29 million passengers flew on Canadian airlines, compared to only 12 million in 1970. The total number of kilometres flown increased from 18,600 million to 48,800 million over the same period.

(Sources: Energy, Mines and Resources Canada; Statistics Canada; Environment Canada)

Problems with transportation don't stop with the individual. Our market economy dictates that, if it is cheaper to import a product from another location than to produce it locally, it is therefore worthwhile to transport that item to market. Perfectly good local products then sit beside similar products imported from thousands of kilometres away. The transport (to market or disposal) of a potentially dangerous product is one of the riskiest stages of the process, and huge volumes of such materials clog our highways and air and sea lanes. Dow Chemical Canada alone transports 2.5 million tonnes of chemicals by rail and another 1 million tonnes by truck annually.

Acid Rain

So much has been written about acid rain in the last decade that it is now part of most people's vocabulary. The burning of fossil fuels, in smelters, in automobile engines and elsewhere, produces a number of environmentally harmful chemicals, primarily sulphur dioxide and nitrous oxide. When these chemicals encounter water, they can increase its acidity.

Acidity is measured with a pH scale and can range from totally acidic (vinegar is a mild acid) to totally basic (lye is a strong base). Most life is adapted to tolerate a small range of variation in the neutral, or middle, part of the scale. When precipitation that has been exposed to sulphur dioxide, nitrous oxide or some similar chemical, falls to Earth, its acidic nature makes the soil and water more acidic.

As lakes acidify, many of the small aquatic life forms die off. This removes the food source of higher animals, which are then either displaced or die off as well. As soil becomes more acidic, vegetation which draws water from the soil can be damaged or die. Acid rain is not only decimating lakes in eastern Canada, it is also believed to be contributing to a decline in maple trees.

One of the major contributors to the acid rain problem is automobile exhaust. It's ironic to see someone driving a car with a "Stop Acid Rain" bumper sticker. If you are concerned about acid rain, cut down on your driving.

Transportation Tips

There are a number of things you can do to reduce the amount of energy and natural resources devoted to transportation.

1 **Buy locally**
Unless there is a significant difference in quality, always favour locally produced items and locally grown foods over those transported in from other areas.

Often, lower costs of production in other areas or other countries can make goods competitive even after the costs of transportation are added. But if you can get what you need from local producers, why support the use of scarce fuel to bring in a comparable product from elsewhere?

2 Consider alternatives to powered transportation

Walking or bicycling will save fuel, reduce pollution and provide you with exercise. The more people who cycle, the safer it will be for those of us who already get about on two wheels. Similarly, cross-country skiing, hiking and canoeing provide the same recreational benefits as snowmobiles, all-terrain vehicles and power boats – and you are able to enjoy the peace and quiet.

3 Question the necessity of the trip

Before using powered transport – whether for a trip down the street or across the country – ask yourself if the trip is necessary. How urgently do you need something from the store? Can it wait until the next time you go? In the case of business travel, can the work be done as effectively by facsimile machine or conference call? And Sunday sightseeing drives are a luxury our environment cannot afford.

4 Select the most appropriate means of transportation

If you can walk or cycle to your destination, do so. If your destination is served by bus or other form of public transit, use it. If you must take your car, arrange a car pool. Every additional driver who travels as a passenger with you takes one more car off the road. On longer trips, consider going by bus or train instead of by car or airplane.

The Earth Is Getting Car-sick

Roughly 80% of all travel within urban areas involves an automobile. There are almost 12 million registered automobiles and 17 million registered drivers in Canada. Our large geographical area and low population density make the automobile a relatively economical and effective method of transportation. However, automobiles are also one of the most significant sources of pollution, particularly in the urban environment.

Automobile Production

It takes a lot of natural resources and energy to make a car. Your family car might weigh in at around 1,000 kilograms. Its composition depends on the make, but roughly two-thirds will be iron and steel. The balance is plastic, glass, rubber, other metals, fabrics and fluids. When you purchase a new vehicle, you are therefore supporting all of the activities of the manufacturers of the various components of the car and placing pressure on the natural resources that go into it. Minerals have to be extracted and refined to produce the iron and steel. Fabrics, paint, plastics and many fluids are obtained through the extraction and refining of petrochemicals. Rubber must be tapped from trees in tropical countries and imported.

Continual model changes put pressure on consumers to buy the latest version and, despite the fact that new cars are a poor financial investment due to rapid depreciation, millions of people succumb annually. Perhaps it is the desire to have a new toy, to one-up the neighbours or to inject some excitement into their lives. Whatever the reason, the end result is that this unnecessary consumption maintains a tremendously destructive industry.

1 **Consider a used car**

Good-quality late-model used cars are an option worth considering. (Older cars may not have sufficient emission controls or fuel efficiency to satisfy an environmentally oriented buyer.) Used cars usually depreciate more slowly than new cars and thus are a better investment, providing they are in good mechanical condition.

2 Buy a quality vehicle

When purchasing a car, buy the best-quality vehicle that you can afford, be it new or used. The best is not necessarily the most expensive car nor the one with the most bells and whistles. Check consumer magazines and guides available at most newsstands to identify makes and models that are reliable and fuel efficient and provide good value for the dollar.

3 Extend the life of your vehicle

If your automobile gets you from A to B efficiently and in relative comfort, why change? The marginal benefits of purchasing a new model rarely outweigh the environmental advantages of keeping your present car (unless, of course, your present vehicle burns leaded gasoline or has poor fuel efficiency). The costs of buying a new car will also usually be higher than the costs of repairing or refinishing your present one.

4 Reduce the number of vehicles

Many families view a second car as a necessity. It rarely is. By exploring a variety of transportation options, it should be possible to manage quite well with one reliable vehicle. Deciding who gets the car when is a matter for family discussion. Carpooling with neighbours and friends, using public transit, cycling or walking are all options that should be considered before purchasing another vehicle. A second vehicle is an even poorer investment than the first – it's used less, but depreciates at the same rate.

Fuel Consumption

In the 1970s, oil prices increased substantially, scaring the world into conserving oil. Gasoline prices almost doubled between 1977 and 1983, resulting in a drop in demand for gasoline which bottomed out in 1983. Speed limits were reduced on major highways. Smaller, more fuel-efficient automobiles became the norm as people traded in their powerful eight-cylinder gas guzzlers for compact four-cylinder vehicles. The average fuel efficiency of new cars almost doubled between 1973 and 1986, from 16.5 litres per 100 kilometres to 8.4.

Although the technology exists to improve fuel efficiency of cars even further, lower oil prices in the late 1980s have taken away the impetus for fuel conservation. In fact, President Ronald Reagan relaxed the fuel-efficiency requirements for new automobiles in 1988 under pressure from the oil industry and automobile manufacturers. Manufacturers are now looking at creative ways to get around even the present fuel-efficiency requirements as public interest in powerful gas-guzzling cars re-emerges in the wake of renewed confidence in fuel supplies. By 1988, gasoline prices had stabilized at roughly the same levels as 1984, and the demand for gasoline had increased to pre-1983 levels. All the wishful thinking in the world, however, won't change the fact that supplies of oil are finite and will eventually run out.

In 1986, more than 80% of the energy consumed by transportation went to road transportation. Clearly, if we are to reduce the pressure on our non-renewable energy sources, it is necessary to reduce the number of vehicles on the road, use them less and improve fuel efficiency.

1 **Select for fuel efficiency** When purchasing a new vehicle, place fuel efficiency at the top of your list of requirements. The average fuel efficiency of new cars is around 8 litres per 100 kilometres, so you should aim for that as a minimum. It is possible, however, to find cars that use less than 6 litres per 100 kilometres. You won't have to compromise power and comfort to any great degree to get better fuel efficiency. For most of your driving, the power promoted for high-performance cars is illusory anyway. It doesn't really matter what your car is capable of when your average speed will likely be far less than 50 km/h.

2 **Consolidate trips** Making lots of short trips wastes time and energy. Consolidate your errands into one outing, and you will reduce the total amount of travel required – which will save you fuel and time and will reduce pollution.

3 **Organize car pools** If you must use a car for your daily activities, particularly commuting, find friends or neighbours who are going in your direction and

double, triple or quadruple up. The average number of occupants per car during rush hour is invariably less than two. Look around next time you are stuck in traffic.

Pooling may take a little more work, but its rewards are many. A fully loaded, fuel-efficient automobile is almost as efficient as public transit. Fewer cars on the road means traffic moves more smoothly, less fuel is burned and fewer pollutants are introduced into the atmosphere. And you get an opportunity to spend time with friends and relatives.

4 **Turn the engine off** If you know that you'll be staying in one place for more than a few minutes, turn your engine off. Since engines are less efficient when idling, you are not only wasting fuel, you are creating unnecessary pollution.

5 **Be a conservative driver** Smooth acceleration and avoiding fluctuations in speed save fuel. Check your owner's manual or ask at your service station for information on how to improve the fuel efficiency of your vehicle by driving prudently.

Tires

Most natural rubber ends up as tires for wheeled vehicles. Rubber is derived from the sap of the rubber tree, found in tropical regions. Tropical forests are cleared for rubber plantations. In 1987, Canada imported 96.6 million kilograms of natural rubber from a wide range of countries including Indonesia, Malaysia, Singapore, Sri Lanka and Thailand. Synthetic rubbers derived from oil have been developed, but they cannot be used in all situations; nor should they always substitute for natural rubber, which is, after all, a renewable resource. However, catering to the world demand for rubber places great pressure on tropical forests.

Vulcanizing is a process that strengthens the bonds in rubber, causing it to harden. Once vulcanization has taken place, these bonds are very difficult to break down, making disposal or recycling of rubber very difficult. According to Statistics Canada, 28 million automobile tires, 2.9 million belted tires, 1.3 million light-truck tires, 1.1 million tires for buses and heavy trucks, 762,000 tires for off-road vehicles and 715,000 tractor tires were produced in Canada in 1985. All of these will end up in scrap yards once their useful life is over. (Ontario, alone, discards approximately 10 million tires each year.) Since vulcanized rubber does not degrade, mountains of tires can be found in locations around the country.

To make matters worse, rubber cannot be disposed of by burning, since the thick black smoke produced is hazardous and contributes to atmospheric pollution. Tires can be recycled, though. The rubber can be shredded and eventually re-used as a component of asphalt, shoe soles and flooring, and for a variety of other applications.

The True Cost of Gasoline

The price of gasoline does not reflect the full costs of using petroleum resources. If the costs involved in combatting the environmental problems caused by the burning of gasoline were factored into the price, consumers would be much more prudent drivers. Some countries encourage conservation by heavy taxation of gasoline. Canadian oil companies like to point out how much of the price per litre is tax, but it is low compared to what people in other countries pay. The following is a comparison, in Canadian cents per litre, of average 1988 prices for leaded gasoline:

UNITED STATES	30.9	CANADA	47.4	UNITED KINGDOM	80.8
FRANCE	99.8	ITALY	128.3		

(Source: Energy, Mines and Resources Canada)

Try comparing the price of gasoline to the cost of other liquids in use around your home. You will find that soft drinks are more than twice the price per litre, while milk is almost three times the price. A bottle of liquor can come in at more than fifty times the price, and some people pay the equivalent of thousands of dollars per litre for a bottle of perfume.

No wonder there is little incentive for conservation. Obviously, by making energy available so cheaply, we are not pricing it according to its true cost. The higher the price for energy, the greater the incentive to conserve.

1 Extend the lifespan of your tires
Rotate the tires on your car regularly so that they wear evenly. Instead of buying new tires when the old ones wear down, consider having your old tires re-treaded to extend their useful life.

2 Recycle used tires
Does your garage or service station participate in a tire-recycling program, or do old tires end up in a compound or landfill somewhere? Support garages that participate in recycling programs.

Atmospheric Pollution

Since automobiles burn carbon-based fuels, whether gasoline, diesel, natural gas, methanol or propane, their exhaust contains carbon dioxide, which contributes significantly to global warming (see Chapter 2). The only way to eliminate carbon dioxide emissions from automobiles is to replace the type of fuel they use. Some research has been done into electrically powered cars and vehicles that can run on hydrogen. However, neither is likely to be used much in the near future. Cleaner-burning fuels such as gasohol (a mixture of ethanol and gasoline), propane and natural gas are becoming more popular. All, however, are carbon-based. Until alternate fuels are developed, reducing the amount of carbon-based fuel being used is the only option. To do this, we must drive less and develop vehicles that are more fuel efficient.

Automobile exhaust also contains carbon monoxide, lead, nitrogen oxides and particulate matter. All these affect air quality. Nitrogen oxides, in particular, contribute to the acid rain problem (see box). Emission controls have helped to reduce the pollutants in automobile exhaust, but they have not eliminated the problems.

1 Maintain your vehicle
A poorly maintained engine is inefficient. Not only can it consume more fuel than necessary, it can also release more pollutants into the atmosphere. Keep your car's engine well tuned.

2 Burn unleaded gasoline
Despite the hazards associated with leaded gasoline, it is still cheaper to buy than unleaded. Disregard the small difference in cost and switch now – if you haven't already – to unleaded gasoline. Soon you

won't have any option: the federal government's ban on the sale of leaded gasoline comes into effect in December 1990.

3 **Select alternate fuels**
Investigate alternatives to gasoline. A properly tuned diesel engine produces fewer pollutants, and some family cars are built with diesel engines. Gasohol can be used in regular engines and improves performance. It has the added advantage of having "built-in" gasline antifreeze. To switch to propane or natural gas, you need an engine conversion and a separate fuel tank, which reduces trunk space. However, operating costs are reduced.

4 **Avoid air conditioning**
Automobile air conditioners contain chlorofluorocarbons (CFCs), which contribute to ozone depletion (see Chapter 11). When you use an automobile air conditioner, you also reduce fuel efficiency.

Other Components

Automobiles also contribute to other pollution problems. All engines require lubricants, oil, antifreeze, and fluids for transmissions, brakes and steering. In the past, the common disposal practice was simply to pour many of these fluids down the drain, which eventually took them into the water supply. Many of these fluids can now be reprocessed and recycled.

Another automobile component that is hard to dispose of safely is the battery (see Chapter 2). The toxic chemicals contained in automobile batteries can be recycled.

- ***Recycle automobile components***

Automobile oil, antifreeze, batteries and other components can be recycled rather than dumped in our landfills or water. When selecting lubricants and antifreezes, consider recycled products. Support service stations and dealerships that recycle used materials. If yours doesn't, either switch or pressure them to participate.

If you are doing your own automobile maintenance, don't flush used fluids down the drain. Take them to a recycling depot, if one is available, or ask your service station how best to dispose of them.

Road Construction and Maintenance

Canada has more than a quarter of a million kilometres of paved roads. Roads are extremely destructive to the environment, not only in terms of the amount of raw materials that are required in construction, but also in the access they provide to previously inaccessible areas. Sometimes, in assessing the environmental impact of roads into remote areas, we consider only the land that is actually overlaid by the road, ignoring the environmental impact of traffic and increased access.

Sand and gravel are used to lay the road bed. This bed is then topped with either concrete or asphalt. More than 400,000 kilotonnes of sand, gravel and stone are extracted from the Canadian landscape annually. Asphalt is a derivative of petroleum. More than three million cubic metres of asphalt are produced in Canada each year, enough to fill a lake one metre deep and almost two kilometres square. Asphalt has a lifespan of ten to thirty years. Both concrete and asphalt can be recycled.

In the attempt to keep roads as free from ice as possible in the winter months, sand and salt are spread on the surface. To say that this is excessive is an understatement. Approximately 150,000 tonnes of road salt are used annually in Canada. Several winters ago, a councillor in Winnipeg complained that there was enough sand on that city's streets to make a camel homesick.

The use of sand, and particularly salt, has consequences for the environment. Most is blown away almost immediately and ends up on roadsides, lawns and even crops. What is left gets on vehicles and speeds up corrosion, reducing their life expectancy and resulting in increased demand for raw materials to construct new automobiles. Finally, virtually all the sand or salt applied ultimately ends up in water.

▪ ***Does your community recycle road materials?***
Everybody complains about road construction and maintenance, but do you know what your community's policy is on the reuse of old material stripped from roads? Concrete can be broken

up and used in place of gravel in the production of new concrete. Steel reinforcing rods in concrete can be removed and recycled. Used asphalt can also be introduced into the mix for new asphalt.

- ***What is your community's de-icing policy?***

How does your community deal with the problem of keeping streets driveable in winter? What sort of controls are in place to ensure that the sand, salt or other material is applied effectively? Is your community considering alternatives that cause less damage to the environment?

Buses and Trains

Despite growing concern for the environment, the increased costs of purchasing, insuring, parking and maintaining automobiles and escalating congestion on the roads, the use of public transit in the United States and Canada has been declining since the Second World War. Governments say they favour and support mass transportation, but their actions don't always show it. Mass transit services, such as buses and trains, are expected to operate with minimal subsidies, on a user-pay system, while governments subsidize road construction and maintenance, which primarily favour automobile users.

If the true costs of maintaining a transportation network were passed on directly to the people who use the systems, it would be clear which is cheaper and more efficient. The government's failure to recognize this was brought home by Prime Minister Brian Mulroney when he told rail passengers to "Use it or lose it" in 1989. The government's desire to reduce the subsidization of VIA Rail led to massive cuts in service. What was ignored is that *all* forms of transportation are subsidized by governments. VIA's subsidy, though, was visible.

The effectiveness of any form of transportation can be measured by the comparative energy required per passenger seat. Obviously, this depends on use. When buses and trains are operating at near maximum capacity, as they do in rush hours, their efficiency is high. During off-peak hours, their efficiency drops, often to the point that they are no more efficient than single-occupant automobiles. This, of course, reduces their overall average efficiency. One of the major challenges facing public transit managers is meeting the high demand at peak periods while avoiding near-empty vehicles during off-peak hours.

1 **Take the bus**

Other than foot or pedal power, buses are still the safest, cheapest and most efficient method of urban transportation. But they are good only if they are used.

2 **Park and ride**

If your home is not located in an area served by public transit, consider driving to the nearest bus or train stop and parking your car. Taking public transit the rest of the way is better than driving the whole distance.

3 **Consider the train**

Few forms of transportation are as relaxing as the train. When congestion and delays at Pearson International Airport reached crisis proportions in 1988, VIA Rail business from Ottawa to Toronto picked up. If the total transit time from downtown Ottawa to downtown Toronto is included, taking the train is almost as quick as flying. Any difference is more than offset by the train's comfort and lower fares. For longer trips, try a train journey, especially if you aren't in a hurry.

- ***Support your local transit system***

If your community does not offer public transit, why not? If it does, what is its attitude toward the service? Does it encourage people to use it by structuring fares favourably, or does it continually complain about the high level of subsidy?

Airplanes

More people are flying these days, and they are taking longer trips. Cargo transport has also increased, rising from 256 million kilograms in 1970 to 498 million kilograms in 1985. Fuel requirements of airplanes increased by approximately two-thirds over the same period. This increased activity means more fossil fuels are being burned, adding to atmospheric pollution and global warming. More resources are needed to produce aircraft, airports and other support services.

1 **Fly only when necessary**
It is hard to believe that the rapid escalation in air travel over the past decade was caused by a sudden increase in people's *need* to travel. Computers, facsimile machines and enhanced telecommunications are supposed to have made business more efficient, and they should be resulting in a *decrease* in the number of people moving about. When you consider travelling for business, assess whether the trip is really necessary. If you are going for a holiday or visit, consider alternate forms of travel such as trains, buses or ships.

2 **Fly efficiently**
Probably the furthest thing from the air traveller's mind when selecting a flight is the fuel efficiency of the aircraft. But all airplanes are not alike in this regard. As with buses and trains, the relative efficiency of aircraft is a function of the number of passengers carried.

Canadian Airlines International Limited publishes the fuel requirements of its fleet. A DC-10 consumes about 40 litres of fuel per hour per seat, while Boeing 767s and 737s require about 30. Obviously, efficiency decreases with more empty seats. In contrast, the smaller DeHavilland Dash-8 uses about 10 litres of fuel per hour per seat. So, on a short haul like Montreal to Toronto, flying in a Dash-8 is more efficient – and it takes about the same length of time.

Moving About Efficiently

Nobody is suggesting we return to horse-and-buggy days, but if we are to avoid being hypocrites, we must examine closely our reliance on powered vehicles. Our roads destroy habitat, both directly and indirectly; millions of tonnes of raw materials are formed into cars annually, just to supply the Canadian market; and operating vehicles utilizes finite resources and pollutes the atmosphere. We should be moving about efficiently, and reducing the amount of fuel consumed and pollution created as much as possible. It is not easy and it requires compromise, but next time you are stuck in gridlock, you may come to appreciate how ridiculous it is to enclose ourselves in individual steel cocoons to get where we want to go.

4

Saving Our Forests

Forests are more than trees. They are complex ecosystems, essential to the health and well-being of the whole planet. Healthy forests support a diverse array of species, consume carbon dioxide and anchor soils. Of all natural resource industries, forestry is probably the most controversial. The industry is so pervasive, the effects of cutting so visible, and the impact on wildlife and the environment from coast to coast so substantial that bitter disputes result.

Few of the forestry industry's critics are opposed to logging. The debate centres on where, how and for what purpose trees are cut and on the overall management of forests. In theory, forests are a renewable resource, but they aren't always managed that way. Reforestation does not keep up with cutting. Much of the wood that is cut is converted to paper, most of which is used once and then thrown away.

You may be unaware that the forest industry is cutting down *your* trees. More than 95% of our productive forest area is located on Crown land. Like all natural resources in Canada, these forests are owned by the public, with responsibility for their welfare vested in governments. Access to the trees is granted through licence to forest companies, and cutting quotas are established. Usually, the company is required to pay a fee for each tree cut and to contribute to the costs of reforesting the land once the trees have been removed.

When the forest industry was established in Canada, the supply of timber in North America must have seemed endless. Now, however, the end is clearly in sight, and it has caught the forest industry by surprise. Today our forests are under increasing pressure as demand for wood and paper products grows.

FOREST FACTS

- Approximately 438 million hectares, or 44%, of Canada's land mass is forested. Canada contains 10% of the world's productive forests.
- Forestry is our major industry. More than 267,000 jobs directly rely on it.
- Canada is the world's largest producer of newsprint, the second-largest producer of pulp and the third-largest producer of sawn lumber. Wood products account for approximately 14% of Canada's exports by value.
- In 1986, 177,097,000 cubic metres of merchantable timber were cut in Canadian forests. That would provide a solid block of wood one metre deep by more than thirteen kilometres square.
- Canada produced almost 35 million tonnes of pulp and paper in 1985, half of which was exported.
- Almost half of Canada's lumbering activity takes place in British Columbia, while more than two-thirds of the pulp and paper industry is centred in Ontario and Quebec.
- Between 1975 and 1985, 8.9 million hectares of forests were cut in Canada. Roughly one-fifth of this land was replanted or seeded, and the rest was left to regenerate naturally. Forestry Canada estimates that about one-third of the total area cut is not regenerating satisfactorily.

(Sources: Statistics Canada; Environment Canada; Forestry Canada)

Deforestation

When we cut down trees without ensuring that they are being regenerated as fast as they are being cut, we contribute to deforestation. Trees consume carbon dioxide, and every tree we lose is one fewer ally in the fight to reduce the build-up of carbon in the atmosphere (see Chapter 2). Removing trees also removes wildlife habitat, leading to a reduction in the range and diversity of wildlife. Trees also anchor the soil. Some logging techniques, primarily clear-cutting (which removes all the trees on a piece of land), contribute significantly to soil erosion.

The less soil available, the less chance that trees will grow back.

Reforestation is accomplished either through natural regeneration or through direct seeding or planting and cultivation (silviculture). The effectiveness of natural regeneration is affected by the type of logging activity that took place on the land and a multitude of natural factors. Forestry Canada estimates that less than two-thirds of the forest lands left to regenerate naturally actually do so satisfactorily. Tree planting or seeding is not as simple as planting one tree for every one cut. We have to ensure that for every tree cut, *one tree grows to maturity.* Areas treated in this way regenerate only slightly better than those left to regenerate naturally.

While much attention is rightly paid to the destruction of tropical rainforests, here in Canada the number of trees cut each year far outstrips the capability of our forests to regenerate themselves.

Conflicts in Your Forests

All across the country, conflicts over forest use and management are raging. The following are some of the major concerns.

Access to Forest Lands

The shortage of trees in many areas is causing the forest industry to search farther afield, and to build logging roads to open up previously inaccessible areas. The result is an emotionally charged debate over the amount of public land being turned over to forest companies. The industry has responded by promoting the concept of "multiple use." Although the concept works for many activities, like cross-country skiing and hunting, it is not always valid.

One area to which multiple use cannot be applied is the establishment of parks and protected areas that are off limits to the forest industry. Currently, only about 2% of Canada's land mass is so designated. Given that approximately half of Canada is forested and virtually all of it is open to the industry, 2% would not seem like much to give up. Yet the forest industry often opposes the establishment of new parks and protected areas, and covets some existing areas, on the grounds that access to this small percentage of the resources is critical to its health. This is a clear admission of their failure to properly manage the lands and forests to which they have already been granted access.

Reforestation

If you lease an apartment, you are required to ensure that the apartment is in good condition at the termination of the lease. If you don't leave the unit the way you found it, you either forfeit your damage deposit or are sued for damages. The same responsibility is not always placed on the shoulders of forest companies. When they are licensed to operate on a piece of land, the onus for regenerating the forests, and for paying for the restorative activities, is a matter of negotiation. By the industry's own admission, it has not, historically, done a good job of ensuring a supply of wood to sustain its operations into the future.

Monocultures

Another area of conflict, related to reforestation, is the creation of single-species plantations of trees called monocultures. Such plantations become substitutes for real forests, but they are poor replacements for the same reason that a wheat field cannot replace a meadow. Since they contain only one species, all specimens of which are roughly the same age, they represent less genetic diversity than a true forest, support far less wildlife and are more vulnerable to insects and disease.

Logging Techniques

Forest management techniques also generate debate, with the most contentious technique being the practice of clear-cutting. Clear-cutting involves cutting everything on a section of land, whether the trees have commercial value or not. The end result is a huge scar on the landscape littered with the waste of the cutting operation. Although clear-cutting is appropriate in some situations, it results in soil erosion and the destruction of wildlife habitat, not to mention its unpleasant visual effect.

Another practice that causes concern is whole-tree harvesting. In an unlogged forest, when trees die they decompose and provide nutrients which re-enter natural cycles. In most logging operations, the waste undergoes the same process and helps to maintain the fertility of the soil. In whole-tree harvesting, though, the entire tree, branches and all, is removed from the site. Leaving too much behind reduces the rationale for destroying the forest in the first place, but taking it all affects the ability of the forest to regenerate itself.

Pesticide Spraying

Pesticides are used regularly by the forest industry, which considers that every tree whose growth is impaired, or that dies, from pests, insects, disease or competition from other plants is "wasted." Although pesticides are used nearly everywhere forests are managed, it is a particular problem near areas of human habitation, where concerns over human health and water contamination are more focused.

- ***Find out what is happening in* your *forests***

In theory, the supply of timber to meet the present levels of demand for wood and paper could easily be ensured if our forests were truly being treated as a renewable resource. Perhaps the greatest contribution you can make is to find out what is happening in *your* forests. Contact your provincial ministry responsible for forestry and any major forestry companies operating in your area and ask for information.

- ***Support protected areas***

Does your government allow timber cutting in parks and protected areas? Forestry and mining are two of the biggest threats to existing protected areas and the greatest obstacles to the establishment of new areas. Demand that your government set aside parks and protected areas to remain undisturbed by these activities.

Forestry Hot Spots

A number of forestry conflicts make the headlines. While conservation organizations and others work to make our forest industry more sustainable and environmentally sensitive, these sites are where the battle lines are being drawn.

West Coast Old-growth Rainforests

These forests have come to the public's attention through campaigns to protect South Moresby, Meares Island and other sites on the west coast of British Columbia. They are lush forests, home to many species not found anywhere else in Canada, and in some cases the world. The trees – cedar, hemlock, Douglas fir and Sitka spruce – are hundreds of years old and invariably huge. Their size is one of their main attractions to the forest industry, which argues that they are better off cut before they die from disease, insects or age.

Because of their age and complexity, though, once cut, neither old-growth forests nor the wildlife they support are likely ever to be seen again under the present approach to forest management. Regenerated forests are slated for cutting at approximately forty years of age. While we express great concern about the destruction of tropical rainforests, we are doing exactly the same damage to our own rainforests.

CONTACT: Federation of British Columbia Naturalists
Friends of Ecological Reserves
Canadian Nature Federation

Stein Valley

The spectacular Stein Valley is the last unlogged watershed in southern British Columbia. An intense conflict is brewing between the forest industry and conservationists and native peoples over the future of the valley. The Stein has acquired some very high-profile support, and every year the "Voices in the Wilderness" festival brings together entertainers and individuals to celebrate wilderness in the valley.

CONTACT: Federation of British Columbia Naturalists
Western Canada Wilderness Committee

Khutzeymateen Valley

Located north of Prince Rupert on British Columbia's west coast, the Khutzeymateen Valley not only contains magnificent old-growth forest, it also boasts the highest concentration of grizzly bears in the province. Conservationists want to see it become Canada's first grizzly bear sanctuary. (The state of Alaska has three.) A moratorium on logging is in place until studies are completed to determine whether logging and the valley's grizzly population can co-exist.

CONTACT: Friends of Ecological Reserves

Temagami

The Temagami area of northeastern Ontario is home to some of Canada's oldest trees, primarily red and white pine. Although not as lush as the west coast rainforests, these forests are also irreplaceable. Again, an intense debate is raging among the forest industry, conservationists, native peoples and local residents over the use of the land.

CONTACT: Federation of Ontario Naturalists
Temagami Wilderness Society

Northern Alberta

Most of northern Alberta is treed with aspen, which, until recently, was considered a "weed" by the forest industry. Now that techniques have been developed to allow aspen to be processed into paper, Alberta has commenced a headlong rush to exploit this new-found resource. A number of new pulp mills will be constructed and several others expanded. Despite the magnitude of the undertaking – an area of forest the size of Great Britain is affected – little environmental assessment and no public consultation took place before the decision to proceed was made.

CONTACT: Friends of the Athabasca
Alberta Wilderness Association
Rawson Academy of Aquatic Science

The Woods We Use

Domestic Woods

The bulk of Canada's forest activity is centred around the so-called "softwoods" – cedar, spruce, fir, larch, pine and hemlock. Spruce and balsam fir alone account for about 75% of the annual volume of trees cut in Canada. Almost all Canada's stands of cedar, Douglas fir and hemlock are located in British Columbia, while spruce, pine and fir are found in virtually all of Canada's forests. Softwoods are used primarily for construction purposes and paper production. In 1980, approximately 147.5 million cubic metres of softwoods were cut in Canada. Half of that was cut in British Columbia, while Quebec and Ontario accounted for another third.

Hardwoods – poplar, ash, oak, birch, maple and walnut – are found in Canadian Shield country, stretching from the Rocky Mountains east to Newfoundland. In 1979, slightly more than 11 million cubic metres of hardwoods were cut in Canada, mostly in Ontario and Quebec, with a lesser amount from New Brunswick. As the term "hardwood" implies, these woods are strong and durable. They are used for furniture, flooring and plywood.

▪ ***Select domestic woods wisely*** Demand for wood and wood products is causing forestry-related land-use conflicts. Therefore, if you are concerned about the fate of Temagami, it is inconsistent to purchase white or red pine. If western rainforests are important to you, then avoid cedar, hemlock, Sitka spruce and Douglas fir wherever possible.

Imported Woods

Many homeowners prefer to use imported woods, primarily teak and mahogany, for home furnishings. However, our demand for these products from countries located in tropical regions contributes to the pressure on tropical rainforests. Whether the wood comes directly from these forests or from plantations, tropical forest land is still cleared to satisfy the demand.

In 1987, Canada imported 17,100 cubic metres of mahogany and 1.9 million square metres of mahogany veneer, primarily from Brazil, the Philippines and the United States. An additional 43.6 million cubic metres of mahogany plywood came from Indonesia. We also imported 61,200 cubic metres of other "exotic" woods from Brazil, Peru, Malaysia and the United States. In comparison with our domestic production of wood and wood products, this amount is minimal, but it is also unnecessary, since the principal use of imported woods is decorative.

- ***Avoid imported woods***
If you are concerned about the destruction of tropical rain-forests, then woods from those regions, such as teak, mahogany, rosewood and ebony, should not be purchased.

TREE PLANTING

With growing concern about the increase of carbon dioxide in the atmosphere and the rate of deforestation, tree planting is being promoted as an activity that can help address these problems. The planting of trees has long been a symbolic activity and still implies long-term commitment. As with many of the other "environmentally friendly" activities in vogue at the moment, though, tree planting by itself is not a solution to the earth's problems. It can even be criticized as supporting monocultures. However, planting trees is within the reach of every individual, whether or not they own property.

Perhaps the most prominent tree-planting program is that of the Boy Scouts of Canada. Since 1973, Scouts have planted 34 million trees. Planting sites and tree species are selected in consultation with provincial forestry agencies. A portion of the funds raised from donors, who pledge support for the program, is used to fund food, water, sanitation and reforestation projects in developing countries. The Scouts' support for tree planting goes back to the 1920s, and in 1987 110,000 participants planted 2 million trees!

Obviously, the infrastructure of the Scouting movement helps with a project of this magnitude. However, many municipalities and conservation organizations sponsor tree-planting days. Individuals can also do their part by planting trees on their own property. If you want some inspiration, watch the Oscar-winning animated film "The Man Who Planted Trees" by Canadian Frederic Back, or read the book by Jean Giono upon which it is based.

Throwing Trees Away

Except as a structural or decorative material around the family home, it is unlikely that you use much wood, directly, in the course of your daily activities. However, the demand for paper and paper products contributes to the deforestation of Canada. Canada is the major supplier of newsprint to the world, and much of the wood cut in Canada each year ends up in pulp mills for processing into paper.

Paper Production

The processing of wood into pulp and paper requires massive amounts of water and energy. Chemicals are added to the wood, under high temperature and pressure, to break it down. This process, and the number of resulting by-products, makes the pulp and paper industry one of the major contributors to air and water pollution in Canada. The effluent from the mills, which is usually expelled into a river, lake or ocean, causes the greatest concern. No one knows how many potentially harmful chemicals are produced during the pulping process.

Pulp mill effluent contains organic material that provides nutrients to algae, which then flourish. When the algae dies and decomposes, the water is depleted of oxygen, which in turn affects fish and other aquatic life (see Chapter 6). The solid waste from the pulping process contains heavy metals and other chemicals which cause water pollution, and it settles to the bottom where it covers aquatic plants. The impact of pulp mills on fish habitat and the environment is therefore substantial.

Bleaching the Environment

A major criticism levelled aginst the pulp and paper industry is that it uses chlorine compounds to bleach the pulp so that white paper can be produced. Bleach generates a number of harmful by-products, the most notable of which are dioxins and furans, both potentially carcinogenic chemicals. Traces of dioxin have been found in everything from coffee filters to diapers. Environmentalists are particularly determined that no new mills using this technology should be allowed to proceed, and that established mills should be converted to less damaging processes. A strong consumer demand for paper produced from "environmentally friendly" pulping processes will help provide the impetus for the industry to upgrade its operations.

CONTACT: Greenpeace

Paper Consumption

According to Environment Canada, Canadians used an average of 4.8 million tonnes of paper per year between 1978 and 1982. Roughly 80% of that paper was used once, then discarded. We may as well construct a conveyor belt between our forests and our landfill sites! Much of the paper is used unnecessarily. Almost two-thirds of the paper that we routinely discard is capable of being recycled, but we are nowhere near that level of performance in Canada.

It is estimated that every tonne of paper recycled, or not consumed, saves approximately nineteen trees. You can do a very rough calculation of the pressure you are placing on forests through the simple act of reading one newspaper per day. Your daily newspaper, depending on where you live, weighs in at 150 to 200 grams. If you read only one paper daily, assuming 300 editions per year, you will consume more than 50 kilograms of newsprint, or approximately one tree, in the course of a year.

The cost of this activity is subsidized by the sale of advertising in the newspaper, but, at fifty cents per copy, your annual cost would be

$150, or approximately $3.00 per kilogram of wood. Like energy and water, paper can be provided to you at a ridiculously cheap price (compare it to the price of steak), and, once again, the consumer is divorced from the true costs of providing the product.

This example concerns only your newspaper reading. It does not include all the packaging, magazines, books, tissues, paper towels and other paper products that you consume annually. Your total personal "tree requirement" will depend on your level of consumption. Multiply that by the number of people in this country, and you will quickly see why our forests are under such pressure.

Now look around your home. With the exception of your books, art and photo albums, you will be hard pressed to find any paper that is not designed to be used once and thrown away. You therefore have a tremendous number of options open to you if you want to reduce your paper consumption.

TIPS FOR PAPER CONSERVATION

1 **Read at the library**
North American newspapers are much bigger than those in Europe. Most newspapers recycle their stories, and much of the copy just fills space around the ads. Buying one good newspaper can generally provide you with all the information you need. You can also cut down on the number of magazines you purchase, particularly glossy consumer magazines that exist primarily to promote products. Instead of buying books, consider borrowing from the library, where you will also find copies of the newspapers and magazines you avoided purchasing.

2 **Select alternatives**
Use cloth towels and napkins instead of paper ones, and handkerchiefs in place of tissues. Use china or durable plastic plates in place of disposable paper ones, and glasses or tumblers instead of paper cups.

3 **Buy unbleached paper**
The process of bleaching paper introduces potentially dangerous pollutants into the environment. Buy unbleached paper products, especially those for which visual appeal is not important, such as toilet paper, paper towels and tissues.

4 Use paper products wisely

When writing, use both sides of a sheet of paper and save used paper for notes, shopping lists, etc. Similarly, if you are photocopying or printing something, do it two-sided.

5 Re-use paper products

Lunch bags can be re-used several times before they wear out. Magazines and books can be shared with friends and relatives, and unwanted copies can be donated to book fairs for resale or to doctors' offices, hospital waiting rooms and so on. You can re-use old envelopes by crossing out the previous addresses. It doesn't look pretty, but most people pay more attention to what's inside.

6 Put paper out for recycling

All paper is not the same, and not all is suitable for recycling. Follow the instructions of your local recycling agency closely. Putting the wrong material into recycling bins increases costs to the recycler, who must pick out unwanted items. Even if your community has no recycling program, there may be local industries that will accept, and maybe buy, your used paper.

7 Buy recycled paper products

Most paper contains some recycled fibre, but try to purchase paper with as much recycled fibre as possible, especially if the quality of the paper is not important. The cost may be a little higher than for paper using virgin material, but if recycled products don't gain consumer acceptance, all the recycling programs will be for naught.

8 Start recycling programs

The potential for paper recycling is enormous. Other countries are far ahead of Canada. If your community doesn't have a recycling program, call for one. You can also start similar programs in your workplace.

9 Lean on manufacturers and newspaper publishers

Contact newspapers, stationery manufacturers, packaging companies and other businesses that use vast amounts of paper and ask whether they use recycled paper in their production processes. If they do, support them; if not, lean on them. There's no point in creating a large supply of recycled paper if manufacturers refuse to use it.

Paper Recycling

Recycling is gaining steam across Canada. But, believe it or not, despite phenomenal public support, there is a definite downside to recycling. In and of itself, it is not the solution to our environmental woes, and it can give us a false sense of accomplishment. The root of the problem is the demand for paper. Unless that demand is stabilized or reduced, recycling will not take pressure off our forests. It will merely reduce the rate at which the pressure is growing. By all means, support existing recycling programs and advocate the creation of new ones, but don't view recycling as an end.

Another problem is that the market for recycled paper is currently weak. We've all seen newspaper reports of entrepreneurs sitting on mountains of paper because no one will buy it. Industries and consumers are still resistant to recycled products. This resistance must be overcome if recycling programs are to be successful. It is also frequently more expensive for industries or consumers to purchase recycled material, giving a competitive advantage to industries that use virgin material. Financial incentives are required to allow recycled products to compete on an equal footing.

Save Our Forests

Not only do we depend on forests for a wide range of goods, forests also consume carbon dioxide, which is accumulating in our atmosphere; they anchor soils, prevent soil erosion and protect rivers, streams and lakes from siltation; they are home to wildlife; and they provide recreational opportunities. Protecting forests is therefore in the interests of everybody and of all life on the planet. It has been left to the forest companies and governments for too long. We all need to reduce the pressure we are applying to forests and to speak up and become involved in the use and management of our forests.

5

Digging Up the Earth

Mining, like forestry, has a significant impact on the Canadian landscape and economy. The major difference is that metals and minerals, unlike trees, are a non-renewable resource. We can plant trees for future generations, but we cannot grow new metals and minerals. Once existing reserves are used up, the only source of supply will be to recycle existing materials, which may or may not be possible, depending on the material and the use to which it was put. Our demand for these materials must therefore be seen from this long-term perspective.

Mining affects the environment in a number of ways. Roads to mine sites destroy wildlife habitat and make it easier for people to get to wilderness areas. Extraction of minerals requires large amounts of energy. So, too, does smelting or refining and the transporting of ore and refined products. Smelting and refining contribute to both air and water pollution. Mine sites and deposits of waste rock also cause water pollution. And to develop new mines, human settlements may be established in areas where they would otherwise not exist.

Since the primary use of most metals and minerals is structural (for buildings, vehicles, appliances, etc.), individually we don't use much metal or many minerals on a daily basis nor do they account for a very large component of household waste. However, every new building, vehicle or appliance does require new supplies of metal. Our demand for more and improved products places great pressure on these resources. To meet this demand, industries are forced to increase capacity and search farther afield for new sources of materials.

Every time you purchase a product made with metals or minerals, you are not only helping to deplete reserves, you also contribute to all of the environmental problems caused by the industry that produced those metals and minerals. For example, if you buy a new car every two years, you are contributing three times as much to the pollution caused by steel mills as someone who buys a car every six years.

In addition to reducing major purchases, we can all conserve metals and minerals on a smaller scale. One way is to recycle metal cans, glass, aluminum foil and a few other things.

We all benefit from the wide range of metals and minerals extracted and refined each year. As with our forests, we all have a responsibility to be aware of how the mining industry operates and to ensure that its products are extracted, refined and used wisely and with minimal damage to the environment.

Mining Hot Spots

While some environmental concerns apply to all mining operations, the following activities or issues are resulting in particular and specific conflicts with the industry.

Uranium Mining

Mining uranium is always controversial. Not only is the use to which most extracted ore is put – generating nuclear power – an environmental and health risk, so is the mining process itself. Uranium ore yields between two and seventy kilograms of uranium per tonne. That means that to produce the 12,437 tonnes of uranium mined in 1987, more than 200,000 tonnes of ore were extracted. The remainder, called tailings, contains concentrations of radioactive material which are slowly released into the environment for hundreds of years. Unless properly treated and contained, these can contaminate air, water and wildlife.

Canada's reserves of uranium are located in northern Saskatchewan, in the eastern part of the Northwest Territories, and in Ontario, north of Lake Huron. The major area of conflict in Canada is in northern Saskatchewan and the southeastern part of the Northwest Territories, with a proposed mine near Baker Lake, Northwest Territories, being of particular concern. This development would occur on the outskirts of

HOW MUCH DO WE TAKE FROM THE GROUND?

In 1987, Canadian mines produced the following:

Sand and Gravel	282,361 kilotonnes	Stone	128,634 kilotonnes
Iron	36,980 kilotonnes	Salt	10,057 kilotonnes
Gypsum	9,949 kilotonnes	Potash	7,399 kilotonnes
Sulphur	5,870 kilotonnes	Zinc	1,482 kilotonnes
Copper	802,181 tonnes	Asbestos	650,000 tonnes
Lead	423,207 tonnes	Nickel	193,391 tonnes
Uranium	12,437 tonnes	Silver	1,452 tonnes
Gold	117,227 kilograms		

• In 1986, the total value of metals extracted from the land was approximately $8.8 billion with a further $2.5 billion generated by non-metallic minerals.

• Approximately 284,000 hectares of Canada's lands are affected by the production of minerals. The majority of this, more than 80%, is used to store the waste that is produced by ore extraction.

(Source: Statistics Canada)

the Thelon Game Sanctuary, one of the largest wilderness areas in the world. Home to spectacular concentrations of wildlife, the Thelon Game Sanctuary is off limits to virtually all human activity, including mineral exploration. However, there are believed to be substantial deposits of uranium within the sanctuary's boundaries, and the industry has placed considerable pressure on governments to allow exploration. Many observers fear that the Baker Lake mine, with the associated investment in support and shipping facilities, will give the industry a toehold in the area that will only add to this pressure.

CONTACT: Canadian Nature Federation
Canadian Arctic Resources Committee
Energy Probe

Northern Mineral Policy

In 1986, Indian Affairs and Northern Development Canada released the Northern Mineral Policy. Its intent was to maximize the amount of land available for mineral exploration in the Northwest Territories. A Conservation Advisory Committee was created to review the status of the Thelon Game Sanctuary, 116 sites identified as important by the International Biological Program but not yet protected, and several federal migratory bird sanctuaries. The committee will recommend whether the boundaries of the Thelon Game Sanctuary and the migratory bird sanctuaries should be modified, and which IBP sites should be protected, in order to determine how much land can be made accessible to the mining industry.

CONTACT: Canadian Nature Federation
Canadian Arctic Resources Committee
Ecology North

Coal Mining

Coal has long been known to be an unclean fuel. Yet the amount of coal used in Canada, primarily for the generation of electricity, has almost doubled in the last decade (see Chapter 2). Most coal is extracted by strip mining, which involves scraping everything off the surface of the land to get at the coal deposit. Large tracts of land are desecrated, and the end result is a huge scar on the landscape. Rehabilitation of the land is rarely effective, and water pollution caused by run-off is a major concern.

In Canada, approximately 27,700 hectares of land are affected by coal mining. Most of Canada's coal reserves are located along the Alberta/British Columbia border, but coal is also found in Saskatchewan, New Brunswick and Nova Scotia. More than one-third of the coal mined each year is slated for export, and it is likely that this amount will grow as industrialized countries continue to demonstrate increasing demands for coal.

Asbestos Mining

Asbestos is considered a significant hazard to human health. The U.S. government, in response to concerns over the environmental and health problems associated with the mineral, is attempting to ban the importation of asbestos. Since most asbestos is mined in Quebec, the Canadian and Quebec governments are lobbying hard to prevent the ban. The annual extraction of asbestos – 650,000 tonnes in 1987 – is substantial, and loss of the industry would have a tremendous economic impact on the local economy. The United States, though, accuses Canada of hypocrisy because we lobby against acid rain, an environmental problem largely imported from the U.S., while at the same time trying to defend the export of an environmentally damaging product to that country.

Mining and the Environment

The mining industry is responsible for much of the air and water pollution in Canada. The extraction, refining and transportation of metals and minerals also consume vast amounts of energy. The following are some of the major environmental problems associated with the industry.

Access

Roads and rail lines built to service mines make previously remote wilderness areas accessible. People also settle in areas where they otherwise would not, further affecting the wildlife and environment of the region.

The mining industry thrives on exploration, and it is pressuring many provinces and territories to allow exploration in parks and protected areas. The rationale seems harmless – exploration can be done with little impact on the natural environment. It is, though, the thin edge of the wedge. It's pretty hard for a government subsequently to deny the industry permission to mine in those areas after it has allowed the industry to go in and look!

Mine Wastes

If nature were simple, you would be able to dig into the ground, find a deposit of a metal or mineral, extract what you needed and then use it. Unfortunately, it doesn't work that way. It is rare to locate a deposit of ore containing a high concentration of the metal sought. Metals or minerals are found in deposits of varying concentration and in combination with other metals and minerals that may or may not be of commercial interest. There may be only a few grams of the metal sought for every tonne of ore. To get at the metal or mineral, huge quantities of ore-bearing rock must be removed from the ground. Some mining techniques, such as strip mining, cause major disruptions to the surface with immediate environmental consequences.

A considerable amount of energy must be expended to separate the desired material from the rock. Only about 2% of the unused rock goes back into the hole. The rest, more than 80%, becomes part of the waste heap. The waste produced in 1981 weighed more than 550 million tonnes. These so-called tailings surround most mine sites, and the vast majority of the land directly affected by mines is used to store the tailings. They are usually quite acidic, and water that passes through them can transfer this acidity to local water supplies. The result is similar to the impact of acid rain (see Chapter 3).

Heavy Metals

Many metallic elements are toxic when they accumulate within the bodies of humans and wildlife. Under natural circumstances, exposure to more than "trace" concentrations of metals such as mercury, lead, zinc and copper is rare. In minute quantities, some of these elements are essential to life, but we are not tolerant of larger concentrations. When ore is extracted from the ground, higher concentrations of these metals enter the environment than would occur through natural processes.

Water filtering through mine tailings can leach out these metals and transport them into a body of water (see Chapter 6). Likewise, smokestacks can introduce them into the air. Since many of these elements are highly toxic to plants, the habitat around mines and smelters deteriorates. Heavy metals also end up in the food chain. Generally, the higher up the food chain you go, the greater the concentration and the more susceptible the animal (including humans).

Smelting

Smelting, or refining, allows metals and minerals to be separated from the ore. Producing the heat necessary requires a tremendous amount of energy. The fuel used by smelting operations is invariably coal, which is one of the dirtiest fuels available. Consequently, smelter smokestacks cause significant atmospheric pollution and are some of the major contributors to the acid rain problem (see Chapter 3).

Smelters also require substantial amounts of water. By-products from the smelting process, including toxic chemicals, cause water pollution. Applying environmental controls to smelters is made difficult by the fact that many mining towns exist solely because of the mine and smelter. Anything that drives up costs and affects the profitability of the mine has immediate repercussions on the economy of the whole town, if not the region.

Imported Metals and Minerals

One of the metals we encounter frequently is aluminum. Although many aluminum products are manufactured in Canada, no deposits of aluminum are located in this country. Aluminum is found in ores called bauxite and alumina. More than 4 million tonnes of this ore were imported in 1987. Most alumina comes from Australia and Jamaica. Bauxite comes from South America and West Africa. Similarly, manganese, which is used in steel production, is not found in Canada. Almost 81,000 tonnes were imported in 1987, principally from Africa.

Obviously, the energy expended in transporting this quantity of metal, or ore, to Canada is substantial. And, by using these products indiscriminately, we are also contributing to the environmental problems of mining in the source countries.

▪ ***How does your province or territory regulate mining?*** Contact major mining companies active in your region and your provincial ministry responsible for mining. What environmental regulations are placed on the mining industry? What steps have been taken to curtail the pollution caused by mines? Are there plans in place to further improve environmental protection in mining operations? What is the policy on mineral exploration and extraction in protected areas?

Metal Recycling

Many metals can be recycled. Steel manufacturers regularly add scrap to the mix, for instance. It is estimated that each tonne of steel recycled saves three tonnes of natural resources. It takes only one-quarter of the energy to recycle steel that it does to produce new steel, and recycling causes only one-quarter of the water pollution and one-seventh of the air pollution that producing new steel does.

Tin can also be recovered from steel cans, where it is used to prevent corrosion. Recycling aluminum requires only 5 to 10% of the energy required to produce new aluminum. Substantial savings can therefore be realized by recycling metal products. Many companies, such as Alcan, are rapidly moving to establish recycling programs.

Reducing Use of Metals and Minerals

The most useful thing we can do to reduce the energy consumed and the pollution produced by the extraction, transport and refining of metals and minerals is to use these products wisely. Metals and minerals are not a significant component of household waste, but, since they are a non-renewable resource, we should not be wasting any of them.

1 Use metals and minerals only where they are necessary

Creating an unnecessary market for a finite resource is not justifiable, no matter how economically profitable it is. A good example is the use of aluminum foil for packaging that could be done equally well with paper, plastic or other material. Try to use materials made from a renewable source rather than a non-renewable one.

2 Get the maximum life out of metal products

Large amounts of iron, steel and other metals are used in the construction of automobiles and appliances. If you usually replace these items before they wear out, you are creating an unnecessary demand for metals, especially since most of the material in the new item will come from virgin, rather than recycled, metals.

3 Support scrap dealers
When you dispose of metal products, take them to a scrap dealer in your area. You will get a few bucks and the dealer will re-introduce the majority of the scrap back into the manufacturing process.

4 Avoid the use of disposable metal
Some products just aren't meant to be disposable (see Chapter 12). Metal products are an example. When you consider the amount of energy necessary to extract aluminum ores, transport them to a smelter, refine them and produce aluminum, does it make sense that the end result should be a pie plate, baking cup or sheet of foil that is used once and then discarded?

5 Favour fresh produce over canned
Fresh fruit and vegetables are far more nutritious than canned ones. The same is true of most other canned products. Buy canned only if fresh produce is unavailable or if you intend to store the food for a long time.

6 Collect used cans for recycling
In many provinces you pay deposits on beer cans to encourage you to return the cans for a refund. You cannot yet do the same for soft drink and food cans, but most recycling programs will accept them. You may also find a scrap dealer in your community who will accept cans for recycling. Many of the major metal producers are also launching recycling programs. They expect to save money by using fewer raw materials, making these programs profitable.

7 Choose glass or fibreglass
Although the production of glass requires a lot of energy, it is one of the more "environmentally friendly" construction materials. Glass, in theory, can be recycled indefinitely. Broken glass, called "cullet," is used to produce new glass; it helps to speed melting of the mix. Glass can also be cleaned, sterilized and re-used many times.

If you have a choice between glass, plastic or metal for a container, glass is best, particularly if the container is designed to be refillable. Similarly, fibreglass is preferable to plastic products in insulation, some structural applications and packaging.

8 Recycle glass
Governments encourage us to recycle glass by requiring that a refundable deposit be paid on refillable glass bottles. Glass containers that are not refillable can either be used for other purposes or recycled. Most recycling programs accept glass jars and bottles, but not broken glass, window glass or ceramics.

Conserving Finite Resources

We know there will come a day, though perhaps not in our lifetime, when many of the metals and minerals we use will no longer be found in quantity in the ground. To put off that day for as long as possible, we have to use metals and minerals appropriately and wisely. A headlong rush to exploit a mineral deposit because there is a market for the product is short-sighted. Most metals, in particular, can be re-used or recycled. Currently, however, it is more profitable for industry to explore for new resources than to invest in recycling.

The impacts of the extraction, refining and transportation of metals and minerals on the environment is probably greater than that of any other industry. Surely it is better for us and for the environment to reduce the consumption of these finite resources, to ensure that they are used appropriately and to increase opportunities for the use of recycled materials.

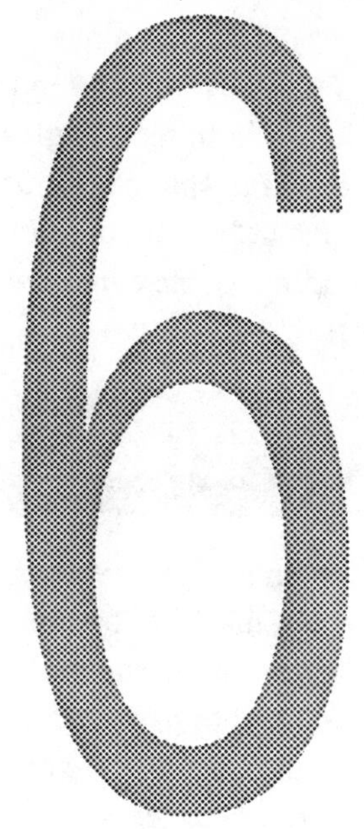

Safe and Plentiful Water

We are all aware that water is essential to life on earth, yet most of the time we act as though supplies of clean, fresh water were unlimited. Recently, many Canadians have begun to question their previous confidence. Droughts have shown how quickly our supply of water can be used up. And even readily available water is, we have learned, not always clean and pure. Residents in many areas – even some relatively large centres, such as Kitchener/Waterloo – have encountered unsafe drinking water.

Canadians use approximately 4 billion cubic metres of water each year. That's more than twice the amount contained in Lake Ontario. By far the greatest proportion of water is used by industries for processing, cleaning and cooling. Individuals use water mainly for household activities, and most of the water we use is eventually returned, treated or untreated, to the natural environment.

If we returned water to the environment in the same condition it was in when we took it, the amount we used would not matter as much. But in addition to the unwanted goods, wastes and chemicals that we dump directly in our waters, we also return used water to our rivers, lakes and oceans laden with raw sewage and the vast quantities of chemicals that we use around our homes and businesses.

Because we Canadians are very wasteful users of water, each of us can choose from many ways to reduce the amount we use. The issue of water is vital to our future, and it, more than any other environmental concern, cries out for political action. A strong commitment needs to be made at all levels of government to ensure that Canadians and the environment continue to benefit from clean and abundant supplies of water.

Water Pollution

Canada contains about 10% of the world's fresh water, but much of it is located far from centres of human population. You would think that that fact would encourage us to take good care of the water supplies that we rely upon. It doesn't, and pollution is a growing problem in most parts of the country. As with atmospheric pollution, some despoliation of water is perfectly natural. However, we are rapidly making things worse, causing adequate and clean water for ourselves and other species to be an increasingly scarce commodity. Four things that affect water quality are eutrophication, siltation, dams and chemical contamination.

Eutrophication

Eutrophication is the natural death of a lake or water body. Human activities are accelerating this process in many areas. When phosphorous and nitrogen, which provide nutrients for algae, are introduced into water through run-off of fertilizers, use of synthetic detergents and release of untreated sewage, algae growth can explode. When the algae die, they sink to the bottom and decay. This rotting matter provides a favourable environment for bacteria. The decomposition process that follows consumes oxygen from the water, reducing the ability of the water body to support other forms of life. Fish and other aquatic life die off, and other animals which feed on them are either displaced or die also.

Siltation

Soil carried downstream in a fast-flowing river or stream settles to the bottom when the speed of flow diminishes. The soil covers vegetation on the bottom, alters the patterns of water flow and affects water quality. Siltation is normal, but poor agricultural practices, the clearing of land and deforestation all contribute to excessive siltation by increasing soil erosion.

Dams

Dams are constructed for flood control and irrigation, for the generation of hydroelectric power or for both. Reservoirs are created behind the dam, flooding the land and inundating wildlife and wildlife habitat. As the flooded vegetation decomposes, it contributes to eutrophication, and it becomes difficult to maintain water quality in reservoirs. The fluctuating water flows downstream from dams also affect vegetation and wildlife. And since most hydroelectric projects are located in northern regions, they have a significant effect on the lives and livelihoods of people who make their living from the land.

Chemical Contamination

Industrial pollution of water attracts much attention because it is usually from a single, concentrated source, such as a factory's effluent pipe, with its unsightly surroundings. Industrial effluent can contribute to eutrophication, the build-up of heavy metals (see Chapter 5) and the introduction of solid waste into the environment. The effects on fish and other wildlife, and their habitat, from these sources of industrial discharge can be devastating. Even if the content of effluent is regulated to ensure that toxic chemicals contained within it do not exceed "acceptable" levels, there may be other effects we don't know about. There are certainly limitations to our knowledge of what can be judged "acceptable." The current goal of environmentalists is "zero discharge" of pollutants, although this may not be feasible for all industries.

Another source of chemical contamination of water is "leaching" of toxic materials into groundwater. Leaching occurs when water is absorbed into the earth. The water molecules can combine with heavy metals and other chemicals they encounter in the soil and can then transport those materials downward into the groundwater. Leaching is of particular concern in areas surrounding mines, hazardous waste disposal sites or landfills.

Water Hot Spots

Conflicts over water use and management in Canada are heating up.

St. Lawrence River

The St. Lawrence is Canada's biggest sewer. Not only is it the conduit through which most of the pollutants from the Great Lakes find their way out to sea, but hundreds of industries and virtually the entire population of Quebec (and many residents of New York state) are doing their bit to add insult to injury. Almost nine out of ten Quebeckers live along the St. Lawrence, and the river is their toilet. In 1985, only 6% of Quebec residents were served by sewage treatment facilities. In addition, industries in the region dump millions of tonnes of chemicals and waste into the river each year.

The symbol of the demise of the St. Lawrence is the beluga whale. Only about 400 of these small white whales remain in the river, and their future is dim. The whales are so inundated with pollutants that their carcasses can be classified as hazardous waste! As mammals, humans are susceptible to many of the problems that afflict the belugas, yet the St. Lawrence remains the source of drinking water for millions of people along the river.

CONTACT: Union québécoise pour la conservation de la nature
Société pour vaincre la pollution

Prairie Water Management

Some people feel that every drop of water that flows downstream past their community is wasted. Two ongoing projects on the prairies, designed to retain water, have ignited strong and vocal opposition.

The Rafferty/Alameda project in southeastern Saskatchewan will dam the Souris River, affecting water flows in North Dakota and Manitoba. Saskatchewan wants to retain water for two purposes: for irrigation and for cooling of a thermal power plant. At full capacity, the reservoir will flood more productive farmland than it will irrigate. There is even a good chance, given regional precipitation patterns, that the reservoir behind the Rafferty dam will never fill to minimum operating capacity. Many believe that if this occurs water may be diverted from the South Saskatchewan River. Critics also wonder why the environment of the region must be destroyed in order to support a coal-fired electricity plant!

A similar conflict is occurring in Alberta, where the government wants to dam the Oldman River, again for irrigation purposes. Opponents have waged a long campaign to protect the river, which is prized for recreation and for its historical significance. A series of court challenges has been mounted, some successfully, but the Alberta government, like its Saskatchewan counterpart, is determined to go ahead.

CONTACT: Canadian Wildlife Federation
Canadian Nature Federation

Water Export

The issue of water export came to the fore during the debate over the Free Trade Agreement with the United States. The catalyst was the GRAND Canal scheme, a project that had a high profile in the early 1980s. Its proponents want to dam James Bay and divert the water southward to increase water levels in the Great Lakes and provide an enhanced supply of drinking water to the United States. The governments of Canada, Ontario and the U.S. have all said that the project will not be considered, but it refuses to go away.

Ensuring Safe Supplies of Water

Depending on where you live in Canada, your water will come from one of four sources: a lake, a river, a reservoir or groundwater. No source is immune from contamination.

Water gets contaminated in a variety of ways. Two of the major sources of pollution are industrial effluent and the leaching of chemicals from the ground, particularly from waste sites. One of the greatest contaminants is human waste, which in almost half of Canada's municipalities is dumped untreated into water. Run-off from storms can also transport pollutants into a water source. In the urban environment, the run-off can carry garden chemicals, road salt and a host of other materials. And the tonnes of animal wastes that are deposited into the urban environment each year eventually end up in water.

Everything you pour down the drain has the potential to contaminate water. Water can be despoiled to various degrees by laundry detergent, cosmetics, household cleaners, motor oils, medicines, paints, solvents and countless other common substances. Sewage treatment is not capable of handling most of these wastes. The cumulative effect of 26 million Canadians' everyday practices is as damaging as any source of industrial pollution. Not surprisingly, many Canadians are beginning to drink their water from bottles.

▪ ***Is your water supply safe?***
Find out where your community gets its water supply. Then try to identify potential threats to that supply. If it is a river, are there any industries upstream that could decrease water quality? Do municipalities upstream discharge their wastes into the river untreated? If you use well water, are there any landfill sites, hazardous waste dumps or other potential sources of contamination in the area? What precautions are taken to prevent seepage and leaching of materials into the water supply?

▪ ***How do industries in your community handle their effluent?***
Do industries in your area affect the quality of water in a nearby region? Do any companies have a history of pollution violations? How tough are regulatory agencies with local polluters?

▪ ***Be aware of hazardous waste dumps***
Wherever chemicals or other potentially hazardous waste are stored, they should be sealed in such a way that the potential for seepage and leaching of chemicals from the site into groundwater, or any other body of water, is prevented. Find out about sites in your region. How closely are they monitored? What is being done to clean them up?

▪ ***How is your community affecting others?***
Does your community discharge untreated waste into the water? How effective is your local sewage treatment plant, if you have one? What plans does your community have to install or upgrade waste treatment facilities?

- ***Make water a political issue*** Write to your municipal and provincial politicians expressing your concerns about water quality. Ask what your local and provincial governments are doing to maintain water quality, both in your community and in other areas that might be affected by activities in your community.

1 Reduce your personal contamination
Cut down on your use of household chemicals and detergents. Don't flush waste chemicals down the drain or sink (see Chapter 10).

2 Use bottled water only when necessary
Concerns over water quality prompt many people to purchase bottled water for drinking. In some areas, of course, this is necessary. While paying for bottled water can encourage conservation, two other factors need to be considered from an environmental perspective. The first is the container, which should be refillable. The second is the energy expended to transport bottled water to market, an unnecessary cost if your local water is safe.

Water Conservation

How much water do you use over the course of a week? The water to make a cup of coffee, to flush a toilet, to take a shower, to do the laundry, to water the lawn, to wash the car and to do the dishes is taken for granted – as long as water is plentiful and clean. In fact, we have become so accustomed to using water without thinking that it is by far our most wasted resource.

In rural areas on the Prairies, where fluctuations in annual precipitation affect the entire economy, water conservation is a way of life. In times of crisis, such as the drought of 1988, urban dwellers in the region (and lately in other parts of the country) are asked to curtail their water consumption. Restrictions or bans are usually placed on lawn watering, car washes and other less necessary uses of water.

If water were more expensive, perhaps its conservation and protection would be easier. Water is so vastly undervalued that there are few

Waste Treatment

Sewage is a major contributor to water pollution. When you flush the toilet, it has to go somewhere. In some municipalities, waste water goes to a treatment plant where some contaminants are removed before the water re-enters the environment. This practice is not as widespread as Canadians might think. Nor is it anywhere near one hundred percent effective. Its success depends on the capabilities of the plant to remove different contaminants, the standards it is required to maintain, and the demands on the system. Some communities have a single sewage system to handle both waste and storm run-off. When run-off increases during heavy rains or thaws, the plant may not be able to keep up with the volume and may return untreated waste to the environment.

Only two-thirds of Canadians are served by sewage treatment plants and fewer than half of Canadian municipalities have some kind of waste water treatment. In contrast, sewage treatment plants serve almost everyone in Sweden, 87% of people in West Germany and 74% of those in the United States. Even communities that do have sewage treatment facilities must still pay attention to this problem. As mentioned earlier, many plants cannot handle the increased demands placed on them or the new chemicals that the plant wasn't designed to catch. In addition, older plants were constructed in times of more lax standards and may not be capable of attaining the environmental standards required today. Many need upgrading or replacing.

restrictions to consumption. Householders in major centres are unlikely to pay more than a few hundred dollars a year for all the water they can use. Some municipalities are moving to a user-pay system, removing the subsidies that have kept homeowners' costs to a minimum. Voters in Calgary, though, recently rejected the installation of water meters, even though they use twice as much water per capita as the people of Edmonton, who have water meters. But even with user-pay systems, so few of the true costs of providing plentiful clean water are incorporated into the calculations that users still get a tremendous bargain.

According to Environment Canada, Canadians used an average of

360 litres of water per day in 1983 at an average cost of $0.25 per cubic metre (one cubic metre equals 1,000 litres). In comparison, the average German used 150 litres daily at a cost of $0.99 per cubic metre. As I pointed out in Chapter 3, gasoline, at slightly less than $0.50 per litre, is undervalued compared to other products. Consider that fresh water, our most precious and increasingly scarce resource, costs approximately $0.00025 per litre in Canada! (In other words, for one cent you can buy 40 litres of water.) But the crunch is coming. Consumers can expect to pay through the nose to construct and upgrade sewage treatment plants in the coming years.

Conserving water isn't likely to affect your pocketbook, since it is so ridiculously cheap. However, as much of the waste of water is unnecessary, neither should conservation adversely affect your lifestyle. Try to equate the use of water with some other liquid. Pretend you are watering your lawn with Scotch, or milk, and see how long you keep the hose on!

CONSERVING WATER IN THE HOME

1 Select the most efficient method of bathing

Baths and showers use varying amounts of water depending on the size of the bathtub, the type of nozzle on the shower and the time spent under the shower. In general, the longer you plan to spend washing, the more efficient a bath becomes. For shorter periods, up to about eight to ten minutes, choose a shower. Showerheads that restrict the amount of water used are available, but a similar effect may be obtained by not opening the tap fully.

2 Use a dishwasher wisely, if at all

Wash dishes by hand, and use the minimum amount of water. If you have a dishwasher, use it only with a full load, and use the economy cycle, if your machine has one.

3 Use your washing machine wisely

Use your washing machine only when you have a full load. The segregation of laundry advocated by detergent manufacturers is designed to increase the sales of their products. Unless you have bright colours that run or sensitive fabrics, it is not necessary to split up your laundry.

4 Watch how much you're flushing

If two litres of water will flush your problems away, four will do it better, right? It doesn't work that way. Toilets in North America are designed to use far more water than those in Europe. You can reduce the capacity of your toilet tank by adjusting the float or placing a large brick or a similar object in the tank. Flush the toilet less frequently. Better still, replace your toilet with one that uses less water.

5 Give your lawn a break

Trees and plants survive in the wild with only rain-water. Your lawn does not require constant watering (see Chapter 8 for more on lawns and gardens). Use a spray nozzle instead of a sprinkler. If you have to stand there, you'll use less water. Try using a watering can instead of a hose for flowers and vegetable gardens. Used dishwater is safe for watering gardens. An old, reliable source is run-off from your eavestrough collected in a rain barrel.

6 Give your car the personal touch

Wash your car by hand using a bucket, a sponge and mild soap. Avoid automatic car washes, but, if you do use them, favour those that recycle their water.

7 Swim in a public pool

Pools are a popular addition to many family homes, but the diversion of all that water to provide recreation for a small number of people is extremely wasteful. The chemicals that are added to pool water also end up flushed down the drain.

8 Observe restrictions on water use

When water shortages hit your community, co-operate with bans on lawn watering and other unnecessary uses. In 1989, an alderman in Ottawa was found watering his lawn during such a ban. *The Economist* recently told of a man in England fined about $400 for a similar violation who, after he sold his story to the media, turned a profit! This cavalier attitude detracts from the seriousness of the issue. Battles have been fought over fresh water, and probably will be again.

9 Be prepared to pay As communities upgrade their sewage treatment plants, the costs are going to be passed along to the consumer. If you adopt conservation practices now, you will be in a better position to deal with price increases in the future.

Protecting Our Most Essential Resource

Compared with other countries, Canada has an abundance of fresh water. In some parts of the world, people walk for miles to get fresh water, and droughts cause mass starvation. Yet here in Canada we take water for granted. We cannot continue to do so. Changing climate patterns and increased demands have created water shortages in most parts of Canada in the last few years. Contamination, with its associated risks to the environment and human health, is a growing problem.

There's no free lunch as far as water is concerned. We are all going to have to start paying a fair price for this commodity. The revenue generated could be used to construct and upgrade waste treatment plants across the country. There will be howls of protest from some segments of the public, but on the issue of water, more than any other, we should be lining up to pay the price, because inaction will be fatal to us all.

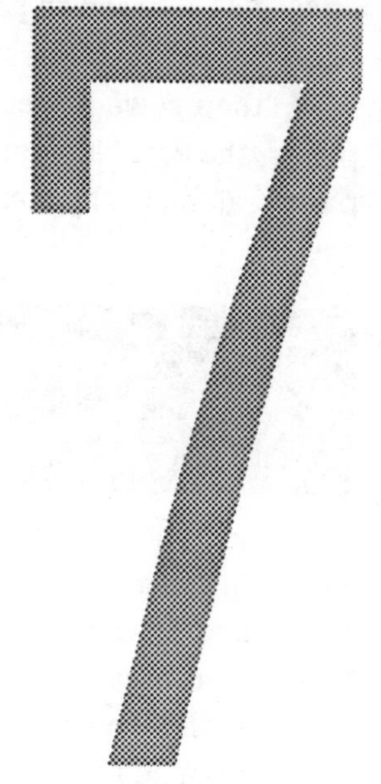

Using Animals and Plants

The manner in which we treat other forms of life is a good indication of our approach to environmental issues and the world in which we live. Part of our concern for the environment comes from a desire for self-preservation. But we cannot solve our environmental problems from such a limited perspective. Progress will come only when we cultivate a respect for all life on the planet.

Our species succeeds at the expense of others. All living beings compete with others for resources. For one to prosper, others must fail. Humans cannot exist on this planet without denying life to other

Animal and Plant Facts

- According to the Canadian Federation of Humane Societies, more than four hundred million animals are used by humans in Canada each year for food, research, entertainment and other purposes.
- In 1981, Canadian farms housed 13,502,000 cattle, 9,875,000 pigs, 92,718,000 chickens, and 9,915,000 other poultry – about five farm animals for each human.
- In 1981, 12.5 million hectares of land were devoted to wheat production, 2.0 million to oats, 1.4 million to canola, 1.5 million to corn, 0.3 million to soybeans and 0.1 million to vegetables. The total cropland was approximately 31 million hectares – almost six times the size of Nova Scotia.
- The number of farms in Canada has declined dramatically since the end of the Second World War, yet food production per capita is increasing.

(Sources: Statistics Canada; Environment Canada)

beings. We can, however, control the degree to which we affect them.

Much of the harm we do to animals, plants and their habitats is unnecessary and wasteful. When we want to, we can be efficient consumers of resources. Wood, for example, is processed into a phenomenal array of products, including fabrics, fuels, drugs, soaps, glues, inks and chemicals. In addition to meat, the hair and hides of animals yield fabrics such as leather, suede, fur and wool. Carcasses can be rendered to produce fats, oils and other materials, and unwanted meat is used to feed pets and other captive animals.

However, we can also be frivolous, particularly toward animals. The antlers, horns, tusks, teeth, claws and shells of many species are used for purely ornamental purposes. While some plants and animals do yield valuable drugs, many cultures erroneously believe that products derived from different parts of animals have (unproven) medicinal powers. Some species of wild animals and birds are in demand as exotic pets. We also use animals for entertainment. We kill them for sport. We ride and train them for rodeos and circuses. We capture them for zoos. And we keep them as pets (see Chapter 8). We also unnecessarily affect habitat by our demand for non-essential products like tobacco, bananas and coffee that require the clearing of vast tracts of land for their production, often in environmentally sensitive areas.

As a highly urbanized society, we have lost touch with the land base that supports us. Food comes from a supermarket, right? Few of us are prepared to look for the source of the food and clothing we use daily. However, one of the greatest pressures on our natural environment results from our demands for food, shelter and clothing. And the greatest abuse of animals and the environment occurs when they are under our direct control.

Eating Animals

Feeding and clothing 26 million people, particularly at the level of consumption we enjoy in Canada, places substantial pressure on our natural environment. The plants and animals we raise for sustenance themselves require nutrients and resources. To provide the volume of products required, farmers have adopted intensive farming techniques designed to get the maximum amount out of the least amount of space. These techniques include crowding animals, using drugs, and applying fertilizers and pesticides to crops.

Most Canadians encounter livestock only at the meat counter of their local supermarket. We react in outrage and deny any personal culpability for the treatment of animals, even if the activity is carried out to satisfy our needs or demands. The animals that end up on our dinner plates have to die, and they don't die of old age. One of the criticisms levelled against those who reproach farmers, hunters and trappers for the way they treat animals is that urban Canadians simply pay someone else to raise and slaughter animals for them and are, therefore, equally responsible for the death of animals.

More than half the grain grown each year goes to feed livestock. The animals digest the grain and convert it, inefficiently, into meat protein. Each of the more than 100 million farm animals in Canada also requires space. If they all roamed relatively freely, farmers and ranchers would need an incredible amount of land. Instead, they crowd the animals together.

Egg producers crowd four or five hens into a small cage where the animals simply become egg-laying machines. Similarly, current poultry

Ethical Treatment of Animals

Debate over the use and treatment of animals centres on two issues: whether the use is justified, and the manner in which animals are housed and treated. Animal rights groups tend to focus on the former, while humane societies or animal welfare agencies tend to address the latter.

Those at one extreme in these arguments feel they can justify any activity as long as there is a perceived benefit to humans and some measures are taken to minimize suffering. Countering this is the "protectionist" argument, which holds that humans have no right to use animals at all, no matter what benefit may result. A more pragmatic approach advocates the three Rs: first, *reduce* the number of animals being used; second, *replace* animals wherever possible; third, *refine* procedures to minimize suffering where animals are used. Where the lines are drawn, of course, depends on the beliefs of the individual.

production favours crowded conditions. One barn can contain thousands of birds. Pigs, which are very intelligent animals, experience a form of boredom when crowded which affects their health and productivity. Often, young piglets will demonstrate the effects of crowding by "tail-biting," chewing the tails of their pen mates. Ventilation is also a problem for pigs. It is not uncommon for the gases that build up in a pig barn to suffocate all the resident animals if the ventilation system fails.

Animals are not machines. Like humans, they are susceptible to stress. Stressed animals are less productive, resulting in lowered profits for the farmer. To counter stress-induced problems and attain maximum production, feed is supplemented with antibiotics to help the animals resist disease. To speed the growth process, diets may be supplemented with hormones. Many of the hormones and antibiotics eventually end up in the food you eat. Adopting more natural ways of reducing stress pays off on the bottom line, and more and more farmers are awakening to that fact.

Like any other commodity, animals may be transported hundreds of kilometres to market. "Acceptable" losses, usually covered by insurance, occur as animals die or are injured as a result of their close confinement in transit.

Support Humane Livestock Practices

1 Visit a farm

While staying at a lodge in the Northwest Territories to view wildlife, my wife and I lived with a native family who told us that every time they went to Edmonton, their kids wanted to see cows! Few urban residents ever take the time to visit an agricultural operation. It is a worthwhile exercise to observe first-hand just how animals are housed and handled. By purchasing meat and other animal products, we are all supporting intensive agricultural practices.

2 Support "free-range" livestock producers

The alternative to intensive farming is the "free-ranging" approach, which, as its name implies, provides much more freedom to the individual animals. This requires more space, energy and labour, but increased productivity of the animals offsets much of the extra cost. Some producers are also enriching their animals' environment by introducing music, toys and other diversions, with similar benefits.

3 Cut down on your meat consumption

You may want to eat less meat out of concern for animal welfare. However, there are other factors to consider as well. Livestock is fed on grain, a major source of protein, and the animals – especially cattle – don't convert that protein efficiently. It is much more efficient for humans to secure their protein directly from the grain than by waiting until it is metabolized into a cow, pig or chicken.

4 Avoid milk-fed (white) veal

The treatment of veal calves is probably the most emotional domestic livestock issue. White, or milk-fed, veal is produced by separating the calf from its mother soon after birth and then confining it in a pen that makes it impossible for it to move around or lie down. The calf is fed a strict liquid diet of milk fortified with nutrients. The result, due to the atrophification of muscles and the rich diet, is an almost white meat that is considered a delicacy by many.

5 Buy your meat from local producers

Buy your meat from as close to home as possible. It is ludicrous to transport a living creature hundreds of kilometres to slaughter, but that is a common practice in Canada. Poorly designed trailers coupled with severe weather conditions and the distances travelled mean that deaths in transit are extremely common, as are injuries. And, of course, the energy expended in transportation is passed on to the consumer in the price of the meat.

6 Buy only what you can eat

When we throw meat away, we are also throwing away all of the resources that went into producing the meat and, more important, showing little respect for the life of the animal. Buy only the amount of meat that you require.

Fish and Seafood

Fish and seafood have long been a diet staple for people in many countries. They are an excellent source of protein, and many Canadians are switching from meat to fish. Now, however, pollution and overfishing have combined to place many stocks in jeopardy. Shellfish in several areas is inedible due to pollution of the marine environment.

Life is not equally distributed throughout the oceans. The greatest concentrations of marine life are found close to shores, where pollution is the worst. Ownership of the best fishing spots is claimed by the nearest nation, and other nations are allowed in to fish under quota. Consequently, prime fishing areas tend to be intensively used. As fish become scarce, conflicts between fishermen and predators increase. Seals and sea lions are particularly singled out, and the killing of these animals is promoted to protect fish stocks.

Wildlife also suffers in some fishing operations. Despite international moratoriums on whaling, some nations persist in killing whales. (Although whales are mammals, whaling has long been considered a fishing activity.) Some fishing nations, in a quest for efficiency, use driftnets, which aren't selective in what they capture, killing a wide variety of marine life in addition to the fish sought. In some areas, tuna school near dolphins, which are then slaughtered when they get caught in tuna nets.

In response to the demand for fish and seafood, a new industry – aquaculture, or fish farming – is booming. Aquaculture operations are cropping up along Canada's coasts and in some freshwater systems. Like agriculture, though, these fish farms affect the local environment substantially. Shoreline habitat is modified, and predator control to protect captive stocks is promoted.

▪ ***How is commercial fishing in your area regulated?***

Of all our natural resource activities, commercial fishing is the least subject to public scrutiny. At present, there is no conservation organization in Canada focusing exclusively on marine issues, and few are involved with freshwater fisheries. Commercial fishing takes place in all provinces. How does your government regulate the industry? How are quotas established? What is the policy on predator control?

- ***Does your government regulate fish farming?*** Aquaculture operations are springing up all over Canada. Few are subjected to environmental assessment, despite their impact on shorelines and the local environment. What is your government's position on the development of aquaculture?

- ***Avoid fish and seafood from countries that fish irresponsibly*** Iceland, Japan and Norway hunt whales, despite international moratoriums on whaling. Japanese, Taiwanese and Korean fishermen use driftnets. By purchasing fish or seafood products from these countries, you are supporting their destructive practices.

Eating Plants

We cultivate only a fraction of the many thousands of species of edible plants in the world. In fact, most cultivated plants are wheat, oats, corn, barley or rice. Monoculture crops (e.g., all wheat or all oats) are more susceptible to disease and attack by insects. Consequently, huge amounts of fungicides, herbicides and insecticides are applied to the land to protect crops. Fertilizers are added to the soil when it runs out of the nutrients needed to produce the same crop year after year. Similarly, we rely on only a few varieties of fruit and vegetables. These crops are treated in much the same way as grains. One of the major uses of chemicals in fruit and vegetable production is cosmetic: to ensure blemish-free produce, all roughly identical in size and appearance, which will be more attractive to you, the consumer.

1 **Support organic farmers**
Organic farmers do not use chemicals. The food produced is usually better for you and better for the environment.

2 **Buy locally**
If the fruit or vegetable you are buying is grown locally, then favour local produce over imported. There's no point expending energy to transport fruit or vegetables if perfectly good produce is available in your region.

3 **Don't judge a book by its cover**
A few blemishes or bruises do not necessarily mean that produce is inedible. Yet we all have a tendency to hunt for the most perfect fruits or vegetables when shopping.

4 **Reduce food waste**
Food wastes may be biodegradable and, in the case of plant wastes, good compost, but wasting food means that all of the energy required to produce the food, transport it to market, package and prepare it has been expended for naught.

Food Production Hot Spots

Intensive Livestock Production

The treatment of animals as a commodity results in overcrowding, stress, disease and a variety of other problems in raising the animals, transport to market and slaughter. Many farmers are now adopting techniques that minimize the stress on the animals and are finding that the increased costs are offset by higher levels of production and reduced losses due to injury and disease. The majority of the millions of livestock used in Canada each year, however, don't yet benefit from that consideration.

CONTACT: Canadian Federation of Humane Societies

Tropical Rainforests

The chapter on forests mentions the reasons for not buying woods imported from tropical regions. But the use of these wood products is

Organic Farming

If modern agriculture spent as much effort trying to learn from nature as it does fighting the natural environment, we'd all be better off. Fortunately, a growing number of farmers are realizing that there must be a better way than today's chemical-intensive methods of growing crops and livestock. These people are practising organic farming.

Organic farmers don't use any drugs or hormones to raise livestock. Their aim in growing crops is to produce and maintain healthy soils. They don't apply chemical fertilizers to crops, and they favour natural methods of pest and insect control.

Depending on where you live, you may find organic produce difficult to locate, but persevere. Such produce may also be a little more expensive, but it is well worth it. Only if people start seeking out and purchasing food from these new agricultural entrepreneurs will organic farming grow and prices come down.

The Mouvement pour l'agriculture biologique produced the Organic Agriculture Directory in 1989. Copies (in English) can be obtained from Les éditions humus, inc., 4545 Pierre-de-Coubertin Avenue, Montreal, Quebec, H1V 2R2 (Tel: 514-252-3039).

only a small component of the pressure that North American society is placing on tropical forests.

The rainforests are being destroyed primarily to clear land for agriculture and settlement. Most cleared land is used for cattle destined for the fast food industry. But many other goods are produced in these regions for export, including coffee, tea, bananas, lemons, cashews, peanuts, cotton, rubber, cocoa and spices. In 1987, Canada alone imported over 324,000 tonnes of bananas from Central America! So, if you are concerned with the escalating pressures on tropical rainforests, avoid purchasing these items.

CONTACT: Probe International
World Wildlife Fund (Canada)

Clearing of Land for Agriculture

As more land is used for agricultural purposes, wildlife habitat is destroyed and less is available for wildlife. One good example is the "pothole." These small areas of standing water are a favoured breeding habitat for waterfowl, but they are an inconvenience to farmers. Farmers continue to drain them, often encouraged by financial incentives, despite the efforts of conservation organizations and government agencies to explain the importance of potholes. Waterfowl populations in North America have plummeted due to the combined effects of drought and habitat loss.

Government subsidies encourage farmers to develop new lands for agriculture. The most acute problem is on "marginal" lands – those areas that are good for wildlife but not necessarily good for agriculture. Accelerated run-off of water from cleared areas contributes to water pollution (see Chapter 5) and, if the areas are burned, air pollution. Prime wildlife habitat is lost in the process.

CONTACT: Wildlife Habitat Canada
Ducks Unlimited

Driftnet Fishing

Some fishing nations, notably Japan, Taiwan and Korea, are waging war on wildlife on the high seas. Driftnets are thin, strong nets up to forty miles long, which, as their name implies, are allowed to drift in the ocean. They capture absolutely everything they encounter. Often, when nets are no longer needed, they are dumped at sea where they continue to ravage the environment for years. If you are concerned about this practice, the best advice is to boycott products from those nations that are culprits.

CONTACT: Greenpeace

Aquaculture

Fish farming is a boom industry. It does not require a lot of space, since thousands of fish can be confined in a relatively small pen. The technical problems these farmers face as they mass-produce fish and other seafoods are quickly being overcome. But conflict over the industry is brewing, particularly in British Columbia, where operations have proliferated along the coast. Unless aquaculture's environmental impact is carefully evaluated, the gold-rush mentality that surrounds the industry at the moment could result in damage to shorelines, fish habitat and the aquatic environment.

Game Ranching

Many agricultural operations are beginning to experiment with new species of livestock. These include a wide range of animals from ostriches to llamas and bison to elk. Each has perceived "advantages" over traditional domesticated species. The greatest conflict is over the ranching of native Canadian wildlife, particularly elk.

Traditionally, wildlife in Canada has been under public ownership. The sale of meat and animal parts has largely been prohibited. Game ranching seeks to make wildlife private property, converting it into a cash crop. The risks associated with large-scale game ranching include transmission of disease to wildlife, control of predators and other wildlife on surrounding lands, damage to vegetation, and genetic manipulation of captive wildlife. If allowed to proceed, game ranching has the potential to change wildlife conservation forever in Canada, not necessarily to the advantage of either the wildlife or Canadians but to serve the interests of a minority of agricultural producers.

CONTACT: Canadian Nature Federation
Canadian Wildlife Federation

Fabrics and Clothing

Fabrics come from three main sources. Wool, silk, leather and suede are derived from animals. Rayon, acetate, cotton and some other fibres are derived from plants. Polyester, nylon, acrylic and other synthetics are produced from petrochemicals. Each of these sources has environmental consequences.

The problems associated with the production of synthetic fibres from petrochemicals are described in Chapter 11. In order for the fabrics derived from plants and animals to become durable and suitable for use, they must be processed, often with environmental consequences. The tanning of leather, for example, results in the release of heavy metal compounds into the environment (see Chapter 5). In addition, fabrics must be dyed (see Chapter 10), which also presents environmental problems. Canada imports a substantial amount of leather – more than 13 million square metres of all forms of leather in 1987. One of the major pressures on tropical forests is the clearing of land for cattle ranches. Canada imports very little beef from Brazil, but we imported over 650,000 square metres of leather from that country in 1987.

More than half of all textiles are cotton. Other common natural plant fibres include rayon, which was the first human-made fibre and is produced from wood pulp or cotton wastes; linen, which is derived from flax; hemp, used in the manufacture of canvas, rope and sacks; and jute, which is used to make burlap. In order to produce plant fibres, farmers employ the same agricultural procedures, such as the use of fertilizers and pesticides, as they use to produce other crops.

- ***Favour natural fibres***

Despite the problems associated with the manufacture of fibres from animals and plants, they have several advantages. They are derived from a renewable resource. Leather and suede are by-products of the use of an animal for another purpose, making more efficient use of the animal. They are also biodegradable. Although the lifespan of fabrics made from some natural fibres may be shorter than that of synthetics, at least when they wear out they can be disposed of. Polyester, on the other hand, stays around (see Chapter 11).

The Fur Debate

Without a doubt, the production of fur is, for many people, the most contentious use of animals. Leather or suede can be viewed as a by-product of an animal killed for food (regarded as a legitimate reason by most people), but a fur-bearing animal is killed solely for its pelt, which is then processed into what many view as a luxury, or non-essential, item. Synthetic furs, promoted as an alternative, are derived from petrochemicals (see Chapter 11) and carry their own environmental cost. A thorough debate of the pros and cons of the fur industry is beyond the scope of this book; however, here are some simple truths.

More than four-fifths of furs come from ranch-raised animals, including mink, fox and chinchilla. These animals are kept in small cages and, in reputable breeding establishments, are relatively well treated considering the circumstances. Poor food and caging, or elevated stress, produces a poor pelt, which defeats the purpose of the exercise. The animals are killed by a variety of methods including having their necks broken, receiving a lethal injection or electrocution.

The vast majority of wild fur is caught in leghold traps. Trapped animals are killed in a variety of ways, including drowning, clubbing and gunshot. The leghold trap itself can cause a great deal of suffering to trapped animals. The oft-heard argument that nature is more cruel is no justification for a human activity. Leghold traps are slowly being phased out in favour of traps that have a greater potential to kill the animal outright. On the whole, however, the fur industry operates today much as it did more than three hundred years ago. Change is coming, but not as quickly as it should.

Trapping is the major source of livelihood for many people in northern Canada, particularly native people. They have little involvement in the more lucrative aspects of the fur industry. Trappers are like farmers: just as only a few pennies from your loaf of bread go to the farmer, so only a minute portion of the price of your fur coat goes to the trapper. The retail fur industry shamelessly accuses anti-trapping advocates of victimizing native people when they themselves have been doing it for centuries. Although the trappers' income from trapping is small, it is vital nonetheless because most of them have few other employment options. And a dollar value cannot be placed on a way of life.

Of greater concern from an environmental perspective is the progressive weakening of our ties with the land. Simply put, the fact that there are several thousand Canadians who make their living from wildlife, and regard these historic activities as an essential component of their culture, is a major aspect in environmental protection. That doesn't mean, though, that people who engage in such activities are above criticism.

▪ ***Think through the purchase of a fur***
The wearing of fur is an emotional issue and more complex than the activists on both sides make it appear. Don't buy a fur as a fashion statement. Examine all aspects of the issue and make your own judgment. You are the one who must live with the decision and, if the debate continues to develop, you are certainly going to have your motives questioned.

CONTACT: World Society for the Protection of Animals
Indigenous Survival International

Product Testing

Another use of animals that generates emotional debate is their traditional role as subjects in medical research and product testing. For hundreds of years, animals have been the preferred tool of scientific research, and many widely accepted and beneficial drugs and medical procedures have been developed using this approach. Today, advances in science have rendered animals inessential for most of the uses to which they are presently put. Cheaper and more reliable alternatives exist in many areas.

The same situation exists with respect to the use of animals to test products. All chemicals intended for use in the home have to be proven safe before they can be marketed. Animal testing has long been preferred for everything from drain cleaner to mascara. The two most common tests are the Draize test and the LD50 test. The former involves applying differing concentrations of the product to the eye of a rabbit (because the rabbit's eye doesn't tear) and assessing its effects by the amount of damage caused. In the LD50 test, animals (usually rats) are fed differing concentrations of product until the concentration that causes half of them to die is identified. This result supposedly gives a relative level of toxicity.

▪ ***Find out what you are supporting when shopping***
Write to the manufacturers of the major household products and medicines you purchase and ask them whether the product is tested on animals. Ask whether the company is actively seeking alternatives or supporting efforts to develop alternate techniques.

▪ ***Are animals dying to make you look better?***
The cosmetics industry has historically been one of the worst abusers of animals. Sacrificing animals for yet another shade of eye shadow is unjustifiable. Find out whether your cosmetics companies test on animals and what they are doing about it. Many are voluntarily moving away from animal testing, but some are digging in their heels.

Personal care products that are not tested on animals can be obtained from The Body Shop, which has retail outlets across Canada, or by contacting Beauty Without Cruelty, c/o South Waterloo SPCA, Box 241, Cambridge, Ontario, N1R 5T8.

Exploiting Wildlife

Former minister of the environment, Tom McMillan, startled delegates to the 1987 meeting of the Convention on International Trade in Endangered Species (CITES), held in Ottawa, when he said that, as far as he was concerned, there should be no legalized trade in endangered species. The international trade in wildlife and wildlife parts is a multi-billion-dollar industry. The illicit trade in wildlife is second only to the illicit drug trade in its size and extent. Needless to say, this exploitation of wildlife is one of the greatest pressures on species worldwide.

Perhaps the most attention has been focused on the rhinoceros and the African elephant, both of which face extinction due to demand for their horn and tusks respectively. Countries like Kenya have made protecting these species a military exercise, and there has been considerable loss of human life as a result. Commercial production is seen as the only way to ensure the elephants' and rhinos' survival. However, demand for live wild animals for pets, zoos, research and so on, and for dead ones for ornaments, furs and "medicines," threatens hundreds of other species from parrots to butterflies to monkeys.

There has always been a segment of our society that demands the exotic. Clothing made from wildlife skins – including alligator shoes, snakeskin boots and exotic furs – is popular, as are jewellery and ornaments made from ivory, tortoiseshell, teeth and claws. Exotic pets are also popular.

Many cultures believe that animal parts have medicinal properties. Oriental medicines are made from products such as antler velvet, bear gall bladders and rhinoceros horns. This demand hits close to home: North America is a major source of antler velvet and bear gall bladders. In some provinces, it is legal for hunters to sell animal parts if the animal has been killed legally. But poachers are doing a lucrative business killing animals illegally just for these products.

1 Don't contribute to the trade in wildlife

Purchasing products such as ivory, tortoiseshell and exotic leathers adds to the tremendous pressures on wildlife, even if the purchase is legal. As society's values toward animals change, such items are likely to be seen negatively rather than as status symbols.

2 Don't purchase exotic pets

Unless a bird or animal has been bred in captivity, each one sold represents a trail of carcasses of others killed during its capture or in transit. Even if the purchase is legal, supporting the keeping of exotic pets only creates demand for them, which encourages the market. Because few people know how to care for these animals properly, many die and others end up in already overburdened animal shelters and zoos.

Developing a Respect for All Life

Our species has succeeded at the expense of other animals and plants, largely those that we have domesticated to provide for our needs. In the process, we have also placed pressure on other species and have developed a very utilitarian approach to nature. We have tended to treat animals in our care as commodities, not as sentient beings.

Taking the shackles off animals, as some animal rights activists advocate, won't necessarily improve life for either the animals or us. To ensure our place on this planet, though, we need to develop a respect for all forms of life, plant and animal. We must keep our use of animals to a minimum, and we must treat those that we do use humanely. In raising plants, we must stop fighting nature and the other creatures that share the environment and start employing nature to our advantage. In all activities we must strive to minimize our disruption of the environment. Only when we achieve these objectives will we truly be part of life on this planet instead of destroyers of life.

8

Nature Around the Home

When we think of nature, wildlife or the environment, we invariably see them as distant from our home and our neighbourhood. Yet nature is all around us, and the way we treat it when it comes into direct contact with us is part and parcel of our attitude toward the natural environment as a whole. Nowhere is this more clearly demonstrated than in our own back yards. Lawns and gardens are nice to look at, but their care involves a manipulation of nature. Farther afield, we have city parks, which provide much-needed green space within communities but implement the same principle on a larger scale. All these efforts to manipulate nature cause varying degrees of damage to the natural environment.

(Lack of) Life in the City

We want nature on our terms, nice and orderly with only the species that appeal to us. When land is developed, the natural habitat is bulldozed. Once houses are constructed, landscapers are brought in to plant lawns, trees and shrubbery, and homeowners create gardens. Any species of plant that is not desired is labelled as a weed and eradicated, no matter how important it might be to the environment of the area.

Some homeowners erect birdhouses and bird feeders to attract the birds that were probably quite common in the area prior to development. Those species that can survive in proximity to humans – such as crows, sparrows, pigeons, raccoons and skunks – prosper. Those that cannot do not return. Some species survive but are viewed as nuisances, and attempts are made to remove them. Nowhere is our mismanagement of the natural environment more evident than in our lawns and gardens.

To make matters worse, homeowners pour tonnes of chemicals and fertilizers on their lawns and gardens annually in an effort to keep grass green, to remove weeds and to destroy insects and other "pests." These chemicals are ingested by wildlife, leach through the soil to groundwater or are flushed directly into sewer systems.

I am not suggesting that we build homes in the woods and let nature have its way with us. Properly managed, the urban back yard can be relatively friendly to the environment and can provide at least a basic habitat for some species of wild animals and plants.

Environmentally Friendly Gardens

Most back yards are sterile places because gardeners tend to fight nature. Look along roadsides and in the surrounding countryside and you'll see plenty of thriving and colourful vegetation proliferating in the absence of supplemental watering and chemicals. Most of it, though, will be "weeds."

If you examined an area of the natural environment in which your community is located, of the same size as your back yard, you would probably find hundreds of species of plants and animals, depending on where you live. In your back yard, you'll find only a fraction of that total, and many of the ones there won't be native to the region. So, by modifying or eliminating the natural habitat of the area, you are contributing to the loss of wildlife in this country. Fortunately, though, it is relatively easy to have an attractive garden and yard and help wildlife at the same time.

1 Make your property chemical-free

Gardeners need to learn the same lessons as farmers, foresters and others: that insects, diseases and "weeds" are here to stay. You can deposit tonnes of chemicals on your yard and it won't make the problems go away. All chemicals do is create the need for more chemicals, and that doesn't do you, your yard, your family, your pets or the environment any good. The best cure is prevention. Mulch, straw or wood chips spread in your garden can inhibit weeds from getting a toehold.

2 Weed by hand

Long before the advent of today's multitude of weed killers, people used to remove undesirable plants from their lawns and gardens by pulling them out by hand. It takes more time, but it's healthier for your garden and you.

3 Use non-powered garden equipment

Use a push mower and till by hand to eliminate the need for gasoline- or electricity-powered garden equipment. If you do use powered equipment, favour electric power over gasoline engines, for the reasons outlined in the chapters on energy and transportation.

4 Compost

Make your own compost pile to produce fertilizer. You will not only reduce the amount of waste that your household throws away (see Chapter 12), you will help your garden. Compost is ultimately far more beneficial to soil than are chemicals.

5 Plant natural species

Plants that are adapted to the environment of your region will do much better than non-native species. That is why "weeds" proliferate. Native plants are also better for other wildlife. Learn what types of vegetation are native to your area and consider planting them in your garden.

6 Consider companion planting

Many plants do better in the presence of some plants and worse in the presence of others. Companion planting places compatible plants together so that each benefits the other by enhancing the soil, by discouraging insects, or in some other way. Tomato plants, for example, benefit plants like lettuce which require the shade the tomato plants create. Carrots and peas also do well when planted together. Gardening in this manner not only makes your garden more productive, it reduces the need for chemical fertilizers.

7 Attract birds
To attract birds you need more than a birdhouse, birdbath or bird feeder. First, determine which species you wish to attract. Then find out what type of habitat and food the species requires and plant appropriately. Shrubs with berries attract many species. Nectar-producing plants and shrubs will attract hummingbirds. Birds also require shelter, such as trees. Each species of bird has its own needs, and species differ around the country. A good field guide or a phone call to your local conservation officer or naturalists' society can provide you with suggestions specific to your area.

8 Take advantage of natural food chains
Everything gets eaten by something. If certain insects are bothering your garden or you, find out what eats them and then take steps to attract those creatures to your garden. Birds consume large numbers of insects. Ladybugs eat aphids, and can be attracted by native vegetation. Many gardeners keep a "weed patch" in the corner of their garden specifically to attract insect predators. By landscaping in favour of certain species of wildlife, particularly birds, you can take advantage of free and natural pest control.

Encountering Wildlife

Some species of wildlife are common in the urban environment. Birds, such as sparrows, crows and pigeons, and mammals, such as raccoons, skunks and squirrels, proliferate because they can survive on garbage and gardens. So-called pests, such as ants and other insects, are also encountered. It is not uncommon for cities and towns, particularly in northern and western Canada, to receive visits from bears, wolves, moose and other large animals that may wander into the area. Although we should strive to provide an environment for wildlife, some species can become a problem and must be dealt with. Larger animals must be handled by wildlife departments or animal control agencies, but homeowners occasionally must deal with smaller visitors.

A Closer Look at Lawns

Nothing symbolizes our myopic view of nature better than the lawn. Many urban conservationists who decry the tendency of agriculture and forestry industries to plant monocultures pursue the very same practice in front of their own homes! Planting a single species of grass and keeping it healthy and pure in the face of everything that nature and the neighbourhood can throw at it is a fanatical pursuit for many people.

Well-kept lawns do look nice. And they are great places to sit and to play. But their environmental cost makes this perfection unworthy of emulation. First, as lawns are a monoculture, the land that they occupy is off limits to the natural vegetation of the area, and cannot support a diverse array of wildlife. Second, lawns are usually made "perfect" by a combination of chemicals, which pollute, and irrigation, which wastes water.

I'm not proposing that you allow nature to reclaim your yard. But a vast expanse of grass is a crime against the environment. There are several ways to get off with a lighter sentence, however. Be creative but, more important, learn to work *with* nature rather than fight it.

For some additional ideas, read the guide entitled "How to Get Your Lawn and Garden off Drugs" available for $12.95 from Friends of the Earth, 251 Laurier Avenue, Suite 701, Ottawa, Ontario K1P 5J6.

1 **Wean your lawn off chemicals** Use natural sources of fertilization, such as manure or compost.

2 **Water your lawn less frequently** Much of the water that you apply to your lawn either evaporates or soaks down through the soil. You can reduce the amount of water applied to the lawn by using a hand-held spray nozzle rather than a sprinkler. It is also more effective to water during the cooler periods of the day.

3 **Landscape creatively** Lawns can be broken up. Intersperse lawn areas with shrubbery, trees and other plants. This diversity can be more aesthetically pleasing and will attract wildlife.

1 Prevention is the best defence

Make sure that there is no way for animals such as raccoons, squirrels and birds to get into your attic, garage or other area where they can hole up. Raccoons can be very destructive, so any screens blocking access should be sturdy. Chicken wire or a similar barrier should be placed around steps and crawlspaces to prevent skunks (or stray cats) from turning them into a den. It is also a good idea to install a screen over your chimney to keep birds out.

2 Avoid chemical control of insects

If you have an insect problem, look for natural means of control. This can involve taking advantage of natural predators or using alternatives to common chemicals (see Chapter 10).

3 Don't panic

As anyone who works in an animal shelter will tell you, the sanest people can become completely unhinged if a bird or animal finds its way into their home. The best way to remove the creature is to open a window or door, close other exits and leave the place quiet. Sooner or later it will find the way out. If the problem is acute, call animal control, your humane society or a conservation officer. (Note: You may get the runaround, depending on the species, but persevere.) Whatever you do, try to keep the animal calm. That is only possible if you keep *your* cool!

4 Don't interfere with nature

We all tend to have a nurturing attitude toward babies. Every spring, when birds are learning to fly and young rabbits and other animals are starting to move about, conservation agencies and humane societies are inundated with calls from people who have found "abandoned" animals. It's hard to walk away, but usually the mother is nearby watching, even though you may not see her.

If you handle the young, it is likely that the mother will reject them. If you do encounter young wildlife, and you are concerned that they may be abandoned, take up a position a considerable distance away and watch. If, after a few hours, you have not seen the mother, then your concerns may be justified. But get advice from a professional before interfering, no matter how cute the young. The vast majority of young wildlife found in this way die anyway, so it is best not to be too hasty in removing them from their environment. Teach your children to follow this advice, too, as children are particularly susceptible to this desire to "help."

Nature in Your Lap

The link between your family pet and the natural environment is not as tenuous as you may think. From a behavioural perspective, dogs are little different from their wild brethren. Cats are domesticated in name only and can quickly revert to a feral state if allowed to run loose. Our attitude toward our pets is a good indicator of our attitudes toward all other life forms on the planet, including other humans.

You don't have to spend much time with a humane society or SPCA to realize the impact that pets, and their owners, can have in the urban environment. A general rule of thumb is that there is at least one pet for every two households, with the great majority of the pets being dogs and cats. So, in a community like Calgary, which has approximately 200,000 households, you would expect to find more than 100,000 non-human residents. Each of these animals has to be nourished and each produces waste, consuming resources and affecting the environment.

1 Your pet doesn't care about the package

One of the most ludicrous aspects of our modern society has been the trend to turn household pets into gourmet consumers. Pet owners are shelling out a fortune to provide their animals with specialty foods, treats, accessories and the like.

Buy the best-quality food you can afford in bulk form. Your veterinarian can help you choose the appropriate brand to ensure proper nutrition for your pet. Avoid especially single servings of canned pet food and those in laminated plastic, paper or metal pouches.

2 "Stoop and scoop"

Nobody likes picking up animal droppings, but tonnes of animal waste are deposited into the urban environment each year by domestic dogs, cats and other animals. Animal waste can contain a wide variety of diseases and parasites, many of which can be transmitted to humans and are particularly harmful to children. Hence, the cleanliness of parks and playgrounds is a very real concern.

Very little of this animal waste ends up in sewage treatment plants where it can be properly dealt with. The rest decomposes and its contents are washed into the local water supply. The relatively simple solution is to take the time to clean up after your pet.

3 Keep your pet under control

Domestic dogs and cats can disturb or destroy local wildlife if allowed to roam unsupervised, and it is difficult for their owners to clean up after them. Owning pets, particularly in an urban environment, is a privilege. With it comes the responsibility of looking after them.

4 Have your pet spayed or neutered

More than 75% of the animals brought to pounds and animal shelters each year are euthanized. Quite apart from the humane and ethical considerations, the carcasses, to put it bluntly, become waste and must be disposed of. This usually means incineration, which causes air pollution, or landfill, which presents problems because the carcasses are pathological waste and pose a health risk. In a city like Winnipeg, about 7,500 surplus pets make the landfill site their final resting place each year. Reducing the number of puppies and kittens being born is one way to solve the problem.

5 See exotic animals at the zoo

Pets have long been a status symbol. Many people seek to differentiate themselves from the norm by owning exotic pets, including tropical birds, monkeys, reptiles, amphibians, big cats and other wildlife species. All these animals come with a hidden price tag. Many are removed from the natural environment for the lucrative pet trade. This is not as simple as it sounds. Nursing mothers may be killed and their young removed; netting methods for birds may injure or kill substantial numbers to obtain stock for trade; and the transport of captured animals can involve considerable distress or even death for the animals in the shipment.

A Note on Animal Control

One of the most emotional debates at the municipal government level centres on animal control. The dogcatcher has traditionally been viewed as a villain when, in fact, effective animal control actually *benefits* pets and pet owners. And cat owners tend to be fanatical about preserving their pets' right to roam freely. What cannot be ignored is that roaming pets are a major social and environmental problem in many communities.

Many pet owners refuse to admit that their animals can do any wrong. But even the most model housecat can terrorize the local bird and small mammal population, further threatening wildlife in the urban environment. Dogs that run loose tend to revert to the packing behaviour of wild dogs. In rural areas, and near urban parks, packs of dogs can pose a great threat to local wildlife, not to mention children. Dogs can kill, and they do it slowly and sloppily, as anyone who has ever seen a deer brought down by a pack of domestic dogs knows.

The solution to the problem of roaming pets is simple. You are the owner. The pet *and its actions* are your responsibility. Keep pets under control and don't allow them to roam freely. Your neighbours, your humane society, wildlife and the environment will appreciate it.

Supporting Nature

Many of us enjoy cultivating lawns and gardens. It gets us outdoors and brings us into contact with other living species. Pets, also, provide contact with non-human species. But nowhere is our misunderstanding of nature, no matter how well meaning, better demonstrated than in the way we treat animals and plants that are in our care. We can berate farmers and foresters for the manner in which we feel they treat nature, but few of us set a good example in our own lawns and gardens, or with our own pets.

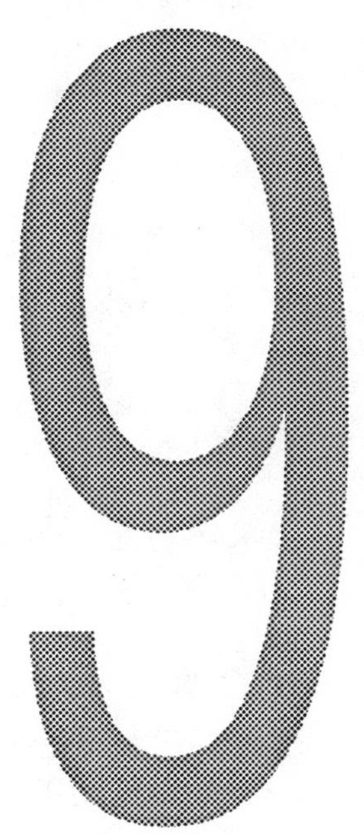

Getting Back to Nature

Despite the fact that we take such poor care of our environment, we still look to nature to provide us with many of our recreational opportunities. These range from facility-supported pursuits, such as golfing and downhill skiing, to motorized activities, such as dirtbiking, snowmobiling and powerboating, to wilderness camping, canoeing and hiking. All affect the natural environment.

The opportunities for some of these activities and the quality of the experience are diminishing as demands on natural areas increase. As a result, people are moving further afield, putting increased pressure on what is left of our wilderness.

Not all recreational activities are appropriate everywhere. Some environments can tolerate very little human disturbance, no matter how benign the activity. For example, as more and more people take to the back country to hike and camp, conflicts with wildlife increase. Many species, particularly large animals like grizzly bears, cannot tolerate the intrusion of humans, even if the humans behave responsibly and place little direct pressure on the environment. Where the conflict becomes acute, it is usually the wildlife that gets the short end of the stick. Too often, the places that most people want to visit are those areas least able to withstand the pressure imposed by the visitations.

Transportation in the Outdoors

Many types of outdoor recreation involve transportation, either as a component of the activity or as the recreational opportunity itself. Powered vehicles such as snowmobiles, power boats and all-terrain

Protecting Wilderness

We tend to see Canada's relative wealth of wilderness as inexhaustible. The truth is that there are few areas of the country left that are still unaffected by human activities. The World Commission on Environment and Development recommends that 12% of a country's geographic area be set aside as parks and protected areas. Canada is barely halfway to this goal – and, if areas that permit logging, mining or hunting are excluded, less than 3% of Canada is truly protected.

Like most labels, the term "park" causes problems. National parks, for example, are set aside to protect representative examples of the different natural features of Canada. To equate them, in title, to the piece of grass at the end of your street is misleading and dangerous. Ironically, the label that is supposed to protect Canada's national parks is itself a threat to them, since, once protected, parks become a magnet for visitors seeking to experience the natural splendours of the area. Increased visitations and the demands placed on services by visitors then compromise efforts to protect the natural environment effectively – the very reason for creating the park in the first place. We need to ensure that only those activities that are compatible with the objectives of our protected areas are encouraged and that the goal of protection should take precedence in all decisions respecting use of the areas.

If Canada is to retain examples of its natural heritage and protect representative areas of different ecosystems, we also need to rapidly complete a national network of protected areas. They don't all have to be national or provincial parks. Other designations – such as ecological reserves, national wildlife areas or migratory bird sanctuaries – can also be made. The important thing is that we get on with the job. Some critics believe that unless we take immediate steps to preserve wilderness, the opportunity will be lost forever within the next few decades, or sooner.

CONTACT: Canadian Nature Federation
Canadian Parks and Wilderness Society
World Wildlife Fund (Canada)

vehicles are popular, but each form of powered transportation has a non-powered equivalent which invariably has less effect on the environment.

To many people, powered vehicles, especially all-terrain vehicles, are the ultimate in freedom. This image is fostered by marketers who show the machines travelling along streams (illegal, by the way) or ripping through rugged landscapes. All across the country, snowmobiles, powerboats and all-terrain vehicles chew up the landscape, directly or indirectly harassing wildlife and other people who are attempting to use the area. I once came across an abandoned four-wheel-drive vehicle, immersed to its windows in mud, in a wildlife refuge in Manitoba. On the east coast, fragile sand dunes are being destroyed by all-terrain vehicles, and efforts to protect the region's endangered wildlife and vegetation are being undermined.

Snowmobiles, powerboats and all-terrain vehicles do have legitimate practical applications, but their recreational use is less defensible. Aside from the manner in which powered vehicles are used, they pose a much more serious pollution problem. All of the problems described in the chapters on energy and transportation apply to these vehicles.

1 Try a non-motorized equivalent

Hiking is an alternative to all-terrain vehicles. Snowshoes and cross-country skis cover the same territory as snowmobiles. Canoes and kayaks will take you to more places than powerboats. These alternatives might not get you where you want to go as quickly, nor with as great a rush of adrenalin. But they are invariably less harmful to the environment, and they provide the opportunity for exercise.

They are also silent, which can greatly enhance your appreciation of the natural environment and provide you with a different type of pleasure. And the only pollution is the extra carbon dioxide you exhale!

2 Leave your home at home

Recreational vehicles are notorious gas guzzlers. What's more, huge recreational vehicles, complete with televisions, are no way to "get back to nature." If you require all the comforts of home, stay in hotels.

3 Use powered transport only when necessary The recommendations pertaining to automobiles in Chapter 2 also apply to the use of other powered vehicles. Since all powered vehicles consume energy and pollute the atmosphere, use them only when there is no alternative.

4 Use powered transportation responsibly Snowmobiles compact the snow, damaging the vegetation underneath. Powerboats generate waves which can damage shorelines and disrupt nesting birds. Off-road vehicles, whether dirtbikes, all-terrain vehicles or four-wheel-drive trucks, make all forms of terrain fair game for wheeled vehicles. And most of us have encountered the idiots who think that harassing other people or wildlife with their contraptions is entertaining! The freedom that these devices give to the user carries with it a responsibility to protect the environment by using the machine appropriately.

Cottages, Trailer Parks and Campgrounds

Every Friday afternoon in the summer, tens of thousands of people join the stream of bumper-to-bumper traffic heading for cottage country or campgrounds. Perhaps the most unusual aspect of this phenomenon is that, once at their retreats, these people invariably create the very conditions they were trying to escape. Cottage communities and campgrounds become crowded and noisy, with traffic congestion on roads and lakes. Often the most relaxing place to spend a summer weekend is a city park, deserted by the hordes who have gone elsewhere!

Having a permanent retreat – whether a cottage, mobile home or trailer – is very attractive to some people. From an environmental perspective, however, the benefits depend on how we manage the land and our activities. After all, such facilities are usually located in an area prized for its natural attractions. Before long, those very attractions can be compromised by our activities: water quality deteriorates, fish and wildlife disappear and the aesthetics of the area are disrupted by human "improvements."

1 Leave natural vegetation intact

Our need to destroy nature and rebuild it on our terms is often carried into the wilderness. Some cottagers clear out the underbrush on their property and often replace it with imported sod and flowers, creating a totally artificial environment. These activities destroy wildlife habitat, resulting, in the long run, in the loss of wildlife from the area (except for those species that benefit from human activities and thrive on garbage, like skunks, raccoons, chipmunks and gulls). If you do modify the vegetation on your property, Chapter 8 provides some advice on how to minimize the effect on wildlife.

2 Protect shorelines and fish habitat

Many cottages are located along the shores of rivers and lakes so the owners can boat and swim. Improperly constructed docks can disrupt water flows and eliminate habitat for fish and other aquatic wildlife. Similarly, removing stones and weeds from the water to create a comfortable swimming area affects fish and aquatic creatures who depend on these for shelter. The result, as with modifications to the land environment, is a reduction in wildlife habitat and therefore wildlife.

3 Handle your waste carefully

Cottage communities rarely have centralized sewage treatment facilities. Cottagers should ensure their waste does not end up untreated in the water supply. If your cottage has inside plumbing, install the best chemical toilet you can afford. Outhouses and septic tanks should be located as far as possible from a shoreline, in order to minimize the risk of leaks contaminating the water.

4 Keep your garbage away from wildlife

Waste-handling facilities in cottage country are generally less elaborate than those in towns and cities. Dumpsites in these areas tend to be magnets for wildlife, such as bears, raccoons and skunks. The suggestions provided in Chapter 12 can help you to minimize your waste at the cottage, but you may have other options in disposal not available at home. If you have a wood stove or fireplace, you can burn much of your combustible garbage. Waste food should be buried, or you can create a compost pile. Hazardous chemicals should be taken back to your home for proper disposal, as should recyclable materials.

Camping – the Better Way

In contrast to cottages and trailers, other forms of outdoor accommodation, such as tents or tent trailers, are cheaper, provide greater flexibility and allow us to get much closer to nature. Similarly, hiking, canoeing and cross-country skiing bring us closer to the surrounding environment. But even campers who eschew all the modern conveniences have to take care that their activities do not damage the environment or mar the experience for others. These "rules" are commonly found on most campground literature but bear repeating here.

1 **Tread lightly**
When camping, particularly in a park or protected area, stick to established trails and campsites as much as possible. Recommended routes and sites can usually be obtained from the authority that oversees the area. Traffic off these trails not only damages vegetation and encourages erosion, it disturbs wildlife. Some promotions have advocated leaving nothing behind but footprints; however, even these can be damaging if left in the wrong places!

2 **Handle your garbage carefully**
All campsites provide receptacles for garbage. Use them and don't leave garbage, particularly food, lying around to attract wildlife. And never feed wildlife – you might be writing their death sentence.

3 **Pack out what you pack in**
On any trips into the wilderness, leave the area you visit in the condition you found it for those who follow you. Many canoe routes and fishing

spots are little more than garbage dumps. The lengths to which some people are prepared to go to get alcohol into the wilderness never ceases to amaze me! You can find beer cans and bottles in the most unlikely places.

4 **Be careful with fire** Fires occur naturally and play an important role in the regeneration of forests. Too little fire is as great a problem for forests as too much. Natural fires, caused primarily by lightning, are started on a random basis. Fires caused by people, accidentally or intentionally, add to the impact of natural fires and result in greater burning of forests than is healthy. And because human-caused fires are usually located close to recreational areas or communities, they are more likely to cause property damage and the loss of lives.

Recreational Use of Wildlife

More and more people want access to Canada's wildlife. In the past, most wanted to hunt and fish. Now, many more want to participate in activities involving nature appreciation, such as bird watching and wildlife photography. While these hobbies place less direct pressure on wildlife (it isn't killed), they can be equally or more damaging to the environment. It isn't unknown for large numbers of bird watchers in single-minded pursuit of a particular species to wreak havoc on the landscape.

Hunting

Fewer Canadians hunt today, and those who do are being forced to move farther afield as more and more landowners close their land to them. While some people welcome this trend, it has a definite downside. Hunters have traditionally been strong supporters of conservation initiatives, contributing substantial amounts of time and money to complement government efforts.

The debate over hunting diverts a lot of attention from more serious environmental issues, although there are environmental consequences to hunting, and hunters are certainly not above criticism. Trophy hunting, for example, which removes the biggest and the best animals from a population, is hard to justify as "conservation." That's like saying that killing Secretariat and using lesser horses for breeding is better for the horse population! Reducing predator populations in order to provide more wildlife for hunters to shoot is also not good conservation.

The fact is, though, that in many areas our activities have driven out natural predators, and humans must now assume that role. As long as populations of game animals and birds are sufficient to withstand the activity, regulated hunting places little pressure on the natural environment.

Fishing

With Canada's abundance of fresh water, fishing is a popular recreational activity, and one that has not yet come under the critical eye of the public. Perhaps because they are not warm-blooded, fish do not evoke the same level of concern as some other species. Even in our national parks, fish are treated differently from other forms of life. You can't hunt or remove any wildlife or plants from national parks, but you can fish in many of them!

The future of Canada's freshwater fish is not rosy. Many accessible lakes have been fished out, and stocking programs have been introduced to restore fish populations. In some parts of Quebec, access to lakes has to be closed in the early morning to control the number of anglers. Acid rain and other forms of habitat destruction are also affecting fish numbers. Consequently, fishing is likely to come under greater scrutiny in coming years.

Wildlife Viewing

Bird watching is one of the fastest-growing recreational activities. More and more people are also taking up wildlife photography. There is a tendency to view these and other activities as more benign than hunting or fishing because they don't result in the death of an animal. However, the increased traffic in natural areas places added pressure on the environment by disturbing wildlife and damaging habitat, regardless of what people are doing. Some of the better birding spots have to be closed once the number of people reaches a certain level. And wildlife viewers can be as irresponsible as other users.

At present, despite the public support for these types of activities, few conservation authorities are expending much effort on promoting them. Most are heavily oriented toward regulating hunting and fishing and producing the species necessary for those activities. Some are now recognizing the opportunity that wildlife viewing provides to develop a much broader constituency for wildlife conservation, and are beginning to respond with programs targeted to these new wildlife users.

1 **Respect the environment that supports your activity** Hunters, anglers, bird watchers and photographers use transportation, make camps and create wastes. It is not enough to catch and release fish, to obey hunting regulations, to get some great photographs or add several birds to your "life list." It is also important to ensure that the environment will continue to produce the wildlife that you seek.

2 **Broaden your horizons** Learn as much as you can about the natural environment of the region in which you are pursuing your activity. The more you know, the better and more enjoyable your experience will be. Then, if you don't catch any fish, shoot any deer or see any unique species, the disappointment may be tempered by an unrelated natural experience.

3 **Obey regulations** Regulations ensure that wildlife is protected for future users. Those who hunt or fish out of season, or exceed limits, jeopardize the future of their activity in that area.

4 **Respect private landowners** We don't have the right to go wherever we want, whenever we want, in pursuit of wildlife. Always ask the permission of landowners before entering their property and respect their wishes pertaining to what you do there.

5 **If you hunt, switch to steel shot** Lead is a known toxin, yet, thanks to hunters, tonnes of spent lead pellets end up in the environment annually. Much of this enters the food chain, affecting a variety of non-game species

as well as waterfowl. The use of steel shot requires an adjustment and a bit of practice, but it is a small price to pay.

6 Report poachers
Some predict that the annual take of wildlife by poachers equals the legal hunt, compromising efforts of wildlife managers and threatening wildlife populations. It is in the best interests of all hunters to report poaching, or evidence of poaching, to the authorities.

7 Catch and release fish
Keep only what you are going to eat and return other fish to the water, providing they aren't badly injured. Using barbless hooks tests the skill of the angler and is a way of landing the fish without causing it undue injury.

8 Keep your distance
In your zeal to get a closer look or a better picture, you can often get too close to wildlife, causing stress to the animals and often making them leave nests, dens or even the area. Keep your distance.

Travel

When you go on vacation to other parts of Canada or other countries, don't take a vacation from your environmental responsibilities. In fact, it could be argued that your obligations increase when you are in somebody else's home. Don't leave anything behind in another part of the world but a good impression, nor take anything away but memories.

1 Carry your environmental ethic with you
Apply the same standards to your purchasing decisions in other locations as you would at home. Many people use travel as an opportunity to relax their standards regarding conspicuous consumption and tend to be more indiscriminate in their shopping habits.

2 Avoid waste in the name of hospitality
Airline food trays end up as plastic waste. Avoid eating on short flights, or take some food with you. Hotels like to make up

Environmental Education

Learning about the natural world is fun and helps you appreciate your surroundings, whether or not you participate in nature-related activities. It also teaches you to be a more environmentally responsible citizen. If you know about the other forms of life that surround you, you may think twice before using chemicals, throwing out too much garbage or consuming excess energy. After all, it is hard to care for what you don't understand.

Fortunately, that understanding is relatively easy to obtain. A brief bibliography is provided at the end of this book. Many libraries and bookstores have extensive sections of nature books. A comprehensive selection is available by mail from the Nature Canada Bookshop, 453 Sussex Drive, Ottawa, Ontario, K1N 6Z4 (toll-free telephone: 800-267-4088). The Nature Canada Bookshop is operated by the Canadian Nature Federation, which also publishes a magazine, *Nature Canada*, that features articles on Canada's natural environment and environmental issues.

You will find provincial naturalist societies listed in Appendix II. Most larger centres have their own naturalists' clubs. The provincial organization will be able to provide you with a contact. These groups run field trips, slide shows, and a wide range of recreational and social activities.

Many communities also have nature centres operated either privately or by governments. These can be excellent sources of information about the local region and provide activities such as field trips and neighbourhood clean-ups. Many continuing education programs are now featuring courses in nature-related subjects also.

There are plenty of resources available to the individual who wants to learn more about the natural environment. All you have to do is pick up the telephone!

rooms every day, replacing towels, soap and other items whether they need it or not. Use your own soap, grooming products and towel.

3 **Avoid wildlife souvenirs** In many countries, wildlife is a cash crop that provides a source of income to local people. However, unless you are sure a product was acquired

legally, do not buy it. The illicit trade in wildlife deals in pets, ivory, furs, leather products, shells, feathers, a variety of "medicinal" powders and solutions, teeth and virtually any part of an animal that you can think of. (Products made from certain species cannot be brought back to Canada anyway. Check with Canada Customs prior to going on your trip to find out what is not eligible.)

4 **Try a nature tour**
Many tour operators are capitalizing on the interest in wildlife viewing and the environment by offering nature tours to other countries. These enable you to learn about the natural environment of other parts of the world and generally offer closer contact with the people than a traditional holiday would. For some ideas, contact Canadian Nature Tours, operated by the Federation of Ontario Naturalists. They can be reached at 355 Lesmill Road, Don Mills, Ontario, M3B 2W8 (telephone: 416-444-8419).

Getting Back to Nature on Nature's Terms

Some of the damage we do to the natural environment is an inevitable consequence of our survival. Some can be justified on an economic or humanitarian basis. But harm we do in the name of recreation or pleasure is not defensible in any circumstances. The more people who experience nature and participate in outdoor recreational activities, the better. It builds a broader constituency for conservation. But let's do it with respect.

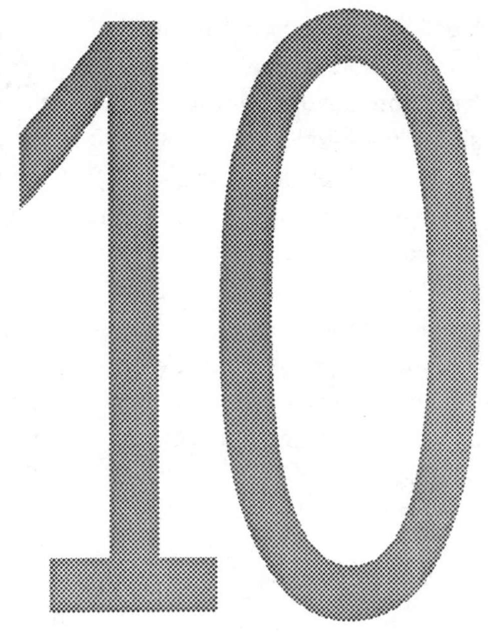

Chemicals and the Environment

Synthetic, or human-made, chemicals have become such an integral component of our daily lives that we take them for granted. We use them to clean, disinfect, dissolve, heal, colour, preserve, deodorize and kill. A fire in the fall of 1988 at a storage facility for hazardous wastes in St. Basile le Grand, Quebec, galvanized Canadian concerns about the storage and disposal of chemicals in this country. The chemicals in the Quebec fire were polychlorinated biphenyls (PCBs), which are suspected of causing cancer in humans. The irony of the situation is that Canadians willingly use chemicals every day that can be as hazardous as, or more hazardous than, PCBs.

Tonnes of chemicals enter the environment through normal household and industrial activities. Most are relatively invisible and accumulate slowly in water, air, wildlife or humans. Hazardous waste dumps become targets for concern, but the vast majority of chemicals do not end up in such sites.

Household Chemicals

Few of us have rusting, fuming steel drums lying around our houses or gardens. But when we think of hazardous chemicals, that is the image that comes to mind. Yet virtually any chemical can pose a hazard if it is used incorrectly, applied in too high a concentration, inappropriately combined with other products or disposed of improperly. Some of the most obvious potentially hazardous products are solvents, drain cleaners, paints, polishes, insecticides, automobile fluids and medicines – products that traditionally bear warnings on their labels.

In addition, many common chemical products in use around the home, which have traditionally been considered more benign, may also

Types of Chemicals

There are two types of chemicals: those that are built on the carbon atom are *organic*; those that aren't are *inorganic.*

Organic Chemicals

Carbon is one of the most versatile elements, and organic chemistry is capable of producing more than a million different chemicals, all based on the carbon building block. Most of these do not occur naturally; they are produced through human manipulations. Because all life, including the human body, is carbon-based, many organic chemicals can react with chemicals within living systems, causing potentially serious effects. Exposure to certain organic chemicals can result in genetic mutations, birth defects, cancers and other health-related problems. For example, exposure to benzene, a component of petroleum, is known to cause cancer and other human health problems.

Inorganic Chemicals

Those chemicals not built on carbon are called inorganic. There are far fewer of these. Some of the major environmental concerns surrounding them are those associated with heavy metals, such as lead (see Chapter 5), those that can provide nutrients for lower organisms, such as phosphates (see Chapter 6), and those that contribute to atmospheric pollution, such as some compounds of sulphur or nitrogen (see Chapter 3).

pose environmental hazards. These include detergents, soaps, shampoos and other grooming products. All eventually end up down the drain, where they accumulate in the water supply. Care must therefore be taken in the use and disposal of *all* chemicals.

Ozone Depletion

Ozone is a form of oxygen. There are two conflicting portrayals of this chemical in environmental reporting, which can lead to confusion. In urban areas, a build-up of ozone is associated with air pollution. In fact, ozone levels are used as an indicator of air quality. In this case, too

What Is Toxic?

When hazardous wastes or other chemicals are the focus of media reports or environmental campaigns, they are often given the labels "toxic," "carcinogenic," "deadly," "poisonous" or some other sinister appellation. The public, rightly concerned about health and safety, reacts with anger, dismay and some degree of paranoia. Labels, however, need to be properly applied. In the case of chemicals, they are not always used correctly.

Every chemical, including water, can be toxic to humans. Whether it is or not depends on the chemical, its concentration and the length of exposure. Some chemicals are dangerous only if one consumes or is exposed to massive amounts over a long period of time. Others can be deadly in brief exposures to small concentrations. Toxicity is, therefore, relative. Labelling a substance toxic, without qualifying the label, doesn't tell the public anything.

much ozone is bad. Yet, at the same time, campaigns are under way to stop the thinning of the ozone layer!

Found approximately 35 kilometres up in the atmosphere, the so-called ozone layer is a band containing high concentrations of ozone molecules. Oxygen normally exists in diatomic form – two atoms bonded together. When the ultraviolet rays from the sun encounter oxygen, this bond can break and the single oxygen atoms may re-combine in a triatomic form, which we call ozone. Ultraviolet radiation can cause ozone to break up again and re-form oxygen. The constant transition from oxygen to ozone to oxygen again absorbs a lot of ultraviolet radiation that might otherwise get through to the surface. One effect of ultraviolet radiation is skin cancer in humans.

Some chemicals introduced into the atmosphere, most notably the chlorofluorocarbons (CFCs), which are found in plastic foams, refrigerators and automobile air conditioners, also react with ozone. Lessening of ozone in the upper atmosphere allows increased levels of radiation to get through, with potential consequences to human health. One irony of the situation is that the industry uses CFCs because of their stability and safety compared to other gases that could be employed for the same purpose – a good example of how the hidden costs of products may not become evident for many years after their adoption.

How Much Household Cleaner Do We Use?

In 1984, Canadian manufacturers produced 189,531 tonnes of granular detergent, 66,500 tonnes of liquid soap and 59,400 tonnes of dishwasher detergent. They also made 16,200 tonnes of scouring powders, 20,200 tonnes of toilet cleaners, 4,300 tonnes of floor polishes, 4,160 tonnes of drain cleaners and 46,371 tonnes of other household cleaners. Guess where it all ends up?

A wide range of ingredients went into these products. Approximately 32,000 tonnes were acids, including hydrochloric, phosphoric, and sulphuric acids. Twenty-two thousand tonnes of chlorine, 37,200 tonnes of detergent alkylates (the base of synthetic detergents) and 38,000 tonnes of phosphates were used. An incredible 179,000 tonnes of sodium-based products, primarily sodium hydroxide (caustic soda), were used in the manufacture of cleaners and soaps.

Household Cleaners

We are a culture obsessed with cleanliness. Certainly, it is important to be clean, but there is a limit to our need for "new, improved" cleaners and other chemical products. When buying food items, you can check the list of ingredients on the package label. In that way, you know exactly what you are getting for your dollar and can make comparisons. Try doing the same thing with grooming and household cleaning products. You will have little luck finding lists of ingredients, although a few products list a guaranteed amount of an active component. The reason is that the competitive marketplace considers product formulas to be trade secrets. No one is going to tell you what makes up your furniture polish, perfume, shampoo or drain cleaner. You are expected to trust the manufacturer and regulatory agency. You have no way of knowing for sure whether a product is new or improved, nor can you compare it with others for its environmental consequences.

The consumer is therefore at a serious disadvantage. Luckily, though, there is a way out. Alternatives exist to almost every type of cleaning product. These generally perform just as well, and are far less damaging and less expensive.

1 Choose soaps over synthetic detergents

Soaps are made from fat or fatty acids and are therefore relatively natural. Synthetic detergents, on the other hand, are artificial and not readily broken down by bacteria, and thus cause water pollution. People washed themselves and their clothing with natural soaps for generations before the advent of synthetic detergents. Let's start doing so again whenever possible.

2 If you use detergents, select environmentally friendly ones

Select detergents that are biodegradable. Avoid products containing phosphates. Phosphates are used to improve the effectiveness of detergents in hard water, but when they are washed into a river or lake their nutritional value results in an increase in algae, which eventually reduces all life in the water system (see Chapter 6).

3 Look for alternatives to household cleaners

For hundreds of years, people kept their homes clean without modern cleaning products. The following are some less-damaging alternatives to chemical cleaners.

Clogged drains: Try a plunger first. If that doesn't work, hot water and 1/4 cup of sodium bicarbonate should be poured in, followed by a few ounces of vinegar.

Glass and windows: Mix up a solution of one part vinegar to ten parts water.

Chrome and stainless steel: Use flour applied with a dry cloth.

Sinks, tiles, etc.: Sprinkle with baking soda and wipe with a damp cloth.

Disinfectants: Mix 1/2 cup borax in one gallon of water.

Carpets and upholstery: Apply cornstarch, then vacuum off.

Furniture polish: Mix one part lemon juice with two parts vegetable oil. Use natural waxes.

Silver polish: Place in boiling water with baking soda, salt and a small piece of aluminum foil (Source: Environmental Management Institute)

Colouring Agents

Colouring agents and the suspensions in which they are carried can harm both the environment and human health. Most dyes are derived from coal, but some are derived from plants or petroleum.

Products that colour tend to come in two types of suspension, either water or an organic solvent. Water-based products may also contain some organic solvent. As the suspension evaporates, the colour is left behind. Many organic-based products don't readily dissolve in water and therefore require organic solvents, such as thinners, to dilute them. For example, turpentine or some similar product is needed to clean up after the use of oil-based paints.

1 **Choose water-based products** Organic solvents pollute water supplies. When they evaporate they also introduce pollutants into the atmosphere and the lungs of anyone nearby. Try to use water-based paints, inks or dyes whenever possible and apply all such products sparingly and carefully.

2 **Remove paint by hand** Elbow grease is less damaging to the environment than the use of thinners and strippers. Use sandpaper or a scraper instead of chemicals to remove old paint.

Chemical Repellents and Killers

In the effort to keep undesirable species of insects and weeds off our property, we have devised a wide range of general or specific chemical killers. But insects are a resourceful lot. They quickly adapt to insecticides, reducing the poison's effectiveness. More and more chemicals soon have to be applied to achieve the same result, and it isn't long before other life forms can be affected.

1 Use natural methods of pest control

Chapter 8 contains some advice on pest and weed control for your garden. A mild mixture of soap and water, applied to the leaves and then rinsed off, can remove insects from house plants. Keeping food tightly sealed and floors and counters clean can deter ants and roaches, which can be live-trapped if they present a problem. A mixture of baking soda and sugar can also be used to kill roaches. Avoid slow-release insecticides such as fly strips and mosquito coils – the insects won't be the only ones inhaling the vapours.

2 Avoid insect repellents

Reducing the amount of skin exposed to insects is as effective a deterrent to bites as are chemical repellents. Wearing protective clothing can be helpful in times of higher concentration. Cedar chips are an alternative to mothballs.

Cosmetics and Medicines

Since most cosmetics, medicines and personal hygiene products are synthetic chemicals, they should be used and disposed of in as responsible a manner as other chemical products. In no other area, except perhaps food, is packaging as wasteful. However, indeed, in the case of lipstick, the container costs far more than the contents, which are basically castor oil, wax and a colouring agent.

We use many cosmetics and personal hygiene products because we've been convinced that we need them. Manufacturers spend a fortune telling us that their products will make us look, smell or feel a little better. We have also been convinced that every time we have a minor health problem we must take something for it.

We are offered a tremendous range of choices in selecting products. Marketers are definitely selling the sizzle rather than the steak, since ingredients vary little among brands regardless of the price. Shoppers Drug Mart recently complained that the number of products it is expected to stock has increased by 43% over the last eight years. One manufacturer offers 13 different types of toothpaste and another provides 24 types of shampoo and conditioner. Those figures don't even include the different sizes offered for each brand! Similar situations occur with virtually all cosmetics and hygiene and medicinal products.

Few of these products have serious environmental consequences themselves, but the resources and energy used in providing this selection is enormous, especially in packaging, and is largely unnecessary.

1 Use the fewest products possible

Do we really need to have several different cold medications, hair care products, deodorants, perfumes or cosmetics? Try to find the product that performs best for you overall and then stick with it instead of maintaining a large number of specialized products. For example, using one good all-purpose cold medication is better than using a pain reliever, a decongestant and other products separately. It's also safer.

2 Specialty products aren't that special

Many of the specialized products, such as shaving cream, skin cleansers and deodorants, can be replaced with a good soap. Mineral oil can substitute for baby oil.

3 Choose the most direct form of application

Applying cosmetics as directly as possible reduces the amount of waste. Stick deodorants are more efficient than sprays, for example. Follow the general rules for application of chemicals provided at the end of this chapter.

4 Avoid packaging

This recommendation can't be repeated enough. Buy in as large a quantity as you can afford and reject products that contain too much packaging. As ingredients don't change much between brands, or with price, the package and the name are the selling point for most cosmetics and grooming products. One of the most useless products to be developed recently is the toothpaste pump. It dispenses the same amount of paste as the tube but takes up much more space in landfill sites. Many medications now come in "blister" packaging, which uses plastic and metal to contain each pill individually (see Chapter 12).

5 Try "natural" medicines Most health food stores stock teas and other products that can provide palliative effects comparable to many synthetic drugs. These take advantage of the "natural" properties of their base rather than relying on manufactured chemicals. If you don't think they work, consider that many of our most effective medicines in battling major diseases are artificial versions of chemicals first found in plants. These products aren't to everyone's taste, but for minor problems they are worth a look.

6 Don't flush medications Old or unused drugs and medications should be returned to your neighbourhood pharmacy, where they can be disposed of properly. Never flush medications down the toilet or sink.

Dry-Cleaning

Dry-cleaning is a chemical process and can result in significant contamination of the environment. It involves suspending the item of clothing in an organic solvent. In many operations, the solvent is then flushed away, despite the fact that it can be re-used. In the closed-loop process, the spent solvent is recovered and re-used. Dry-cleaning packaging, the thin plastic film in which cleaned items are covered, is also wasteful.

1 Reduce dry-cleaning Dry-clean only those clothes and materials that absolutely require dry-cleaning, and clean them only when necessary. Not only will you contribute less to pollution, you'll save money. Many items can be washed by hand in cold water and hung to dry instead.

2 Check the process Favour establishments that recover and re-use dry-cleaning fluids.

3 Return your hangers If you are accumulating clothes hangers from your laundry or dry-cleaner, return them so that they can be re-used, if you don't need them.

Other Chemical Products

1 **Reduce the use of glues**
Most glues are organic. The fumes that they give off contaminate the atmosphere and may present a health hazard. Glues also affect the ability to recycle products, particularly paper. Perfect-bound magazines (those with hard spines), telephone books, "post-it" notes and other glued paper cannot be easily recycled due to the presence of glue.

2 **Use preservatives and sealants carefully**
Again, these products can contaminate the air through their fumes, and water, should protected products be immersed in or exposed to it. Be careful with wood preservatives, waterproofing chemicals and other sealants.

3 **Avoid deodorizers and air fresheners**
Aerosol deodorants and air fresheners are rarely necessary. Virtually anything that has a pleasant odour can pervade a room and counter other smells. If you want your house to smell of flowers, for example, fresh flowers will do the job.

Effective Application and Disposal of Chemicals

Chemicals are so omnipresent that a comprehensive review of all applications is impossible. There are a number of steps you can take to minimize the environmental impact of virtually all synthetic chemicals around your home, though. The guidelines provided below can be applied to most chemicals.

1 **Explore alternatives**
Before using synthetic chemicals, make sure that their use is necessary and appropriate. If a more natural alternative is available, consider using it.

2 Avoid packaging
Buy in bulk and refill containers instead of purchasing a number of small containers. Packages that contain a combination of materials, such as paper and plastic, paper and metal or plastic and metal, should be avoided.

3 When purchasing potentially hazardous chemicals for a specific purpose, buy only what you need
Suggesting that you buy household chemicals in the smallest possible container seems, on the surface, to contradict recommendations to buy in bulk to reduce packaging. But there's a big difference between pouring a litre of spoiled milk down the drain and a litre of unused turpentine.

If you decide to use a hazardous chemical, such as a wood sealant, for a specific, once-only application, purchase only what you need and apply it wisely. If you have a substantial quantity left over after the job is done, give it to a friend or neighbour who may be performing a similar task. When the container is empty, clean and dispose of it in a safe manner.

4 Apply the product efficiently
Chemicals may be applied in aerosols, sprays, streams, powders, creams, gels, foams or other solid or liquid forms. Choose the method of application that gets the most product to its intended target in the most efficient fashion. Aerosols should be avoided; they are relatively inefficient and the pressurized containers are difficult to dispose of. One of the simplest ways to ensure efficiency is to apply the chemical, such as tile cleaner, directly to the cloth, mop or other applicator, use it until its effectiveness diminishes and then reapply. This method prevents the waste that is associated with applying large amounts of a product and then washing or wiping it off.

5 Use the minimum amount of product
Even if you are applying a product efficiently, whether it is drain cleaner or shampoo, it is still possible to use far more than you require to get the job done. The balance, of course, is washed away. That's not only chemicals going down the drain, it's your money as well! Therefore, it makes sense to use only

what you really need. Manufacturers want you to buy more of their product, so use their recommended quantities as a guide only. You may find that you can get the results you desire by using far less of the product than suggested.

6 **Never mix chemicals**

It's unwise to play amateur chemist. Two relatively benign chemical products can produce a dangerous reaction when mixed, causing a serious hazard to your health and the environment. Don't mix chemicals unless what you are doing calls for a specific formula, then follow the instructions to the letter.

7 **Keep containers safely sealed and secured**

Since you don't want chemicals seeping all over your house, garden or garage, all potentially hazardous chemicals should be securely sealed and stored in a cool, dry location. Keep all such products safely out of the reach of children and pets. For example, many a family pet has died from ingesting automobile antifreeze, which tastes sweet but is deadly.

8 **Don't flush chemicals**

Disposal of chemicals is a bigger problem than getting rid of the container. No problem, you say? Just flush them down the drain? Chemicals disposed of in this manner may be out of sight, but they don't go away. Once a chemical enters the water, it is likely there to stay. Even sewage treatment plants are not designed to remove the multitude of chemicals in use today. Consequently, almost everything you flush down the drain re-emerges in somebody's drinking water, and does environmental damage en route.

9 **Rinse containers before disposal**

Disposing of used containers presents a real problem. The chemicals left inside can leak out once the container finds its way to a landfill site. There, they can be leached into the soil and eventually find their way into a water supply.

Before you throw out a container, try to remove as much of the product as possible from it. For many products, this can be done simply by rinsing the container with a small quantity of water and then applying the slightly diluted contents to whatever you were using the product on before. Clean containers can then be sent for recycling.

10 Participate in hazardous waste disposal days

Wastes that cannot be disposed of in the water supply or a landfill site should be stored safely and then taken to a hazardous waste disposal site. Many communities offer special disposal days when consumers can bring in all of their household hazardous chemicals. These are often so popular that the disposal site cannot handle the volume. If such days aren't offered in your community, push for them.

Responsible Care

In response to growing public concern over chemicals and the environment, the Canadian Chemical Producers Association has instituted a program called Responsible Care which is essentially a code of practice for the industry. The seventy members of the CCPA produced $9.6 billion in chemical products in 1987 and directly employed 23,500 people.

One component of Responsible Care is the establishment of a Chemical Referral Centre. The Chemical Referral Centre is a toll-free, non-emergency telephone service. Operating between 8:00 a.m. and 6:00 p.m. Eastern Time, the centre can provide health and safety information on thousands of chemicals and chemical products. All you have to do is tell them the technical or trade name of the product, and the manufacturer's name if possible.

If you want more information about chemical products found around your home, call the Chemical Referral Centre at 800-267-6666.

Not All Chemicals Are Bad

Much of the environmental rhetoric these days focuses on "chemical" as opposed to "natural" products, leading the public to believe that the two are clearly separated. They are not. Everything is made of chemicals. The distinction arises when we consider synthetic chemicals that are not normally found in the natural environment. Even then, the separation is not clear-cut with respect to environmental or health concerns.

Not everything that is natural is good for you. Arsenic and cyanide, for example, are perfectly natural. Similarly, not all chemicals developed by humans are dangerous. Certainly, no one can deny the improved quality of life that many medications, products and processes have provided to humans.

But with the benefits of chemicals comes the downside. As with other environmental issues, there are no simple answers. We can't condemn all chemicals unthinkingly, but, as we have with other things throughout this book, we must question as much as possible the need for using chemicals. Those chemicals that are found to present serious risks to the environment or human health should definitely be banned. But for many applications the answer lies in using chemicals appropriately and responsibly. There is no need to use a synthetic chemical if a safer, less damaging and equally effective alternative is available. Where chemicals are used, steps should be taken to ensure that the minimum amounts necessary are used and that they are disposed of properly.

The Permanence of Plastics

There are few aspects of our lives that are not touched by plastics. New types of plastics and new uses for them are continually being developed. Plastics have become a universal substitute for paper, wood, metal and other, more natural, products, largely because they are cheaper to produce and use in the short term and are more "convenient." But the fact that they *can* be substituted for these other products is no reason that they *should* be.

The very factors that make plastic products desirable – their low cost, light weight, high strength and durability – are the major reasons that they pose such a major environmental problem. They confer short-term advantages, but their long-term environmental costs may be far greater. Certainly, no other class of products better symbolizes our wasteful society than plastics, particularly the "disposable" variety.

The Source of Plastics

Plastics are derived from carbon-based sources – primarily oil, but also coal or natural gas – and from wood. Approximately 5% of the oil and natural gas extracted annually is used to produce plastics. In Chapter 2, the environmental implications of extracting, transporting and refining these products were described. The same consequences must be taken into consideration when evaluating the use of plastics.

These source materials are refined into petrochemicals, which are then processed into a variety of plastic resins. The resins are then made, singly or in combination, into plastic products and a wide variety of materials, including synthetic rubber and synthetic fibres.

The Plastic Foam Example

Plastic foam products have become a lightning rod for the present-day concern about the environment, largely because of the deterioration of the Earth's ozone layer. Thinning of the ozone layer is attributed, in part, to the effects of CFCs, which are gases that can be used to cause the bubbles in plastic foam products. The polystyrene coffee cup has thus become a symbol of how our unthinking individual actions accumulate to create serious environmental problems.

The depletion of the ozone layer has brought international attention to the issue of CFCs and their application. Many jurisdictions, including several in Canada, have moved to greatly reduce, or ban, the use of these chemicals. Some manufacturers of plastic foam products have voluntarily switched, with much fanfare, to technologies that do not involve CFCs. In the process, as usual, less attention has been given to evaluating whether we need things like foam cups at all.

Although it is commendable for a business to cease using a problematic chemical, consumers should not go overboard congratulating themselves, or businesses, for using "CFC-free" foam products. Plastic foam cups – even without CFCs – still contribute to other, equally serious, environmental problems.

An array of chemicals may be added to the plastic resins to give the finished product different properties. These include colorants, stabilizers (to protect against decomposition due to heat, the ultraviolet rays in sunlight or oxidation), flame retardants, glass (to improve strength) and a variety of other additives.

All plastics are not alike. Each has its own properties, and even types of the same plastic may contain different additives. These differences are one of the major obstacles to recycling of plastics.

Some of the major types of plastic are: *acrylics*, a substitute for glass that is also found as glues and fabrics; *nylon*, the first synthetic fabric to be used widely, made into items ranging from stockings to bullet-proof vests; *polyester*, a fact of life in the clothing industry but also used for plastic films and bottles; *polyethylene*, found as plastic bags, packaging and bottles; *polypropylene*, used for ropes and some fabrics; *polystyrene*, found as either fibres or foam in containers, packaging and insulation; *polyvinylchloride*, or vinyl, used in a wide variety of applications; and others such as *polyurethanes* (insulation), *epoxies* (glue), *alkyds* (paints) and *melamine* (dinnerware).

Plastic Is Not Disposable

Many plastic products have a useful lifespan ranging from just a few minutes to a few days, although there are more permanent applications. Once used, however, the product may remain with us for decades, or longer. Plastic comprises a significant portion of municipal waste by volume, although its proportion by weight is much less. About two-thirds of plastic found in landfill sites will be from products that have a useful life of less than one year. Thus, the amount of landfill space taken up by these "disposable" items is generating increased concern.

One of the misnomers of our consumer society is the word "disposable." In theory, you can throw away anything, making everything from pianos to bricks disposable. In reference to plastics, however, "disposable" means that the product is used only once or twice before being discarded. There is thus no need to clean or store the object, whether it is a razor or a cup.

Recycling

Recycling of plastics is not yet a viable option, although some initiatives have recently been launched. Since each type of plastic has different properties, in order to recycle it effectively, plastic must be properly sorted. Some plastics can be recycled relatively easily, but many cannot. Those that can be recycled are shredded and used to make other plastic products including roofing material, fence posts and insulation. Often, more plastic resin must be added to the mix to maintain the properties desired in the end product. Even if effective, recycling cannot by itself provide the answer to waste problems, although it can be a major component of waste reduction.

Landfill

Most plastics are treated to improve their resilience to attack by chemicals and sunlight, and they are naturally resistant to attacks by biological agents. Therefore, once a piece of plastic is in a landfill site, it stays there for a long time. Although some experts view plastic as "good" landfill, due to its stability, it is better to avoid using up landfill space in the first place.

As landfill space becomes harder and harder to find, particularly in heavily populated areas, the permanence of plastic will be a growing problem. One hundred years from now, an archaeologist may uncover a mountain of lime-green polyester pantsuits and plaid sports jackets. Is that how we want to be remembered?

Incineration

Burning waste plastic efficiently is difficult, if not impossible. Very high temperatures and high levels of oxygen are required to ensure proper combustion. The burning produces toxic gases, and unless the plastic waste is incinerated efficiently, it will produce soot, contributing to atmospheric pollution. The ash left behind may be contaminated by the additives used in plastic production, primarily heavy metals. Although the volume of this residue is less than the original plastic, it presents a different problem for safe disposal.

Plastic Litter

Not all plastic finds its way into the garbage stream. Instead, it is left to litter roadsides, parks, waterways and just about everywhere else. Plastic litter is not only unsightly, and likely to stay that way, it is a significant threat to animals, fish and birds.

Some of the biggest offenders are six-pack rings, balloons and fishing line. When animals become entangled in the plastic debris their movements or breathing may be restricted, often causing death. They can also choke on litter such as deflated balloons. The situation is far worse in the U.S. There, protecting wildlife from such debris is moving closer to the top of the priority list for many conservation and animal welfare agencies.

1 Don't endanger wildlife with litter
Plastic should be put in the garbage. Avoid littering is such a basic piece of advice that it is painful to have to repeat it here. However, the consequences of disposing of plastic products improperly may take years to be realized.

2 Avoid six-pack rings
The plastic rings that hold six cans together simply make it easier to carry the cans. Buy your cans loose or in cartons. If you do buy or find six-pack rings, take the time to snip open all the loops, even if you are disposing of them properly, to ensure they are less of a hazard to wildlife.

3 Don't release balloons
What goes up must come down, and balloons are no exception. They rarely land in the same location where they were released. Tonnes of plastic is introduced into the environment in this way each year and, when it lands, it can pose a threat to wildlife and the environment. If you are going to use balloons, keep the number to a minimum, don't release them, explode them before disposal and dispose of them in the normal waste stream.

CONTACT: World Society for the Protection of Animals
Defenders of Wildlife

Cutting Your Plastic Intake

Plastics should be used appropriately and only when absolutely necessary. A general rule is that the longer the useful lifespan of the product, the more defensible the use of plastic in its manufacture. However, one of the major applications of plastic is for packaging. Some tips for assessing packaging are provided in Chapter 12.

1 Avoid plastic bottles and containers

Glass, paper and metal containers are generally preferable to plastic, particularly if they can be re-used or recycled. Unless you have a well-established recovery program for plastic wastes in your community, the use of plastic containers and bottles should be avoided wherever possible. Most Canadian homes contain dozens of plastic margarine containers that someone intends to re-use but doesn't. If they aren't in your cupboards, they'll be sitting in the landfill.

2 Avoid plastic packaging

Buying your meat from a butcher, fruit and vegetables from a market, and baked goods from a bakery is one way to avoid the plastic foam trays and clingfilm wrapping that supermarkets use to present these foods. Buy eggs in compressed paper rather than foam packages. Since most frozen or processed food comes with a plastic tray and wrapping, try to purchase unprocessed food. Avoid single-serving packages.

One annoying trend of late has been the move to plastic bags as mailers for magazines. These bags are cheaper than envelopes but they aren't doing the environment any favours. The surprising thing is their adoption by many publications promoting environmental protection!

3 Avoid clingfilm

Seal your foods, including those that you "brown bag" for lunch, in durable re-usable plastic containers rather than use clingfilm. Take the containers home and use them again.

4 Avoid fast food outlets

Given Canadian dietary preferences, this could be difficult! However, the volume of garbage produced by these outlets is staggering. For every one of those billions of meals served, somewhere there is a foam carton taking up space in a landfill site. If you do eat at fast food outlets, favour those which package their food in paper.

5 Use durable cups and cutlery

A durable coffee cup, whether it is china, ceramic or plastic, is preferable to a disposable cup. If you buy drinks by the cup, carry your cup with you and ask to have it filled. You might even get a break on the price, since the seller won't have to pay for the cup and lid. Every time you use your own cup, one less polystyrene cup ends up in the waste stream. Similarly, alternatives to plastic knives, forks, spoons, stir sticks and similar items should also be favoured.

6 Wear natural fibres

Polyester, acrylic and nylon are often less expensive than natural fabrics, but their long-term cost is greater. Favour wool, cotton, rayon and other, more natural, fibres. At the very least, look for blends that reduce the amount of synthetics used in the production of a garment or fabric.

7 Use cloth diapers instead of disposables

Babies go through an incredible volume of diapers. Every one of the disposable kind ends up in a landfill site where it will remain for years. In addition, tonnes of untreated sewage are introduced into the environment with the diapers. While there are definite environmental consequences to the laundering of cloth diapers, cloth is still far preferable to "disposables." And you don't have to clean all those soiled diapers yourself; diaper services are competitive with the price of disposables. Most also pick up and deliver – a boon to busy parents.

8 Recycle toys

The toy store is nirvana for plastic lovers. If you buy plastic toys for your children, don't throw them away once the child tires of them. If they are still in usable condition, give them to other children who might enjoy them, or donate them to hospitals or day-care centres.

9 Avoid trinkets and gadgets

The versatility of plastics means that gimmicky items can be mass-produced cheaply and sold for a substantial profit. Once they have provided their few moments of enjoyment or service, they are thrown out. Fads like hula hoops, Rubik's cubes and wall walkers are examples. If you are unable to resist the temptation to try one, ask a friend if you can borrow or share.

10 Re-use plastic wherever possible

Take your own bags to the grocery store. If you refuse bags or use your own, you'll probably get a funny look from the clerk, but in a few years the funny looks will be reserved for the people who ask for bags. Durable plastic containers can be re-used for a variety of other purposes. Be creative!

The "Degradable" Trap

In response to concern about the prevalence of plastics and the difficulties in recycling, many manufacturers are now producing "biodegradable" or " photodegradable" plastics. These terms leave the impression that the action of bacteria (bio) or light (photo) breaks down the product over time into natural components that can then re-enter natural cycles. This is true for some products, but not for plastics.

The strength and durability of plastics is due to their molecular structure: long chains of molecules bound tightly together. These chains do not break down easily. In so-called biodegradable plastics, say a plastic bag, another compound, such as starch, is mixed in with the plastic. Over time, in a landfill or wherever, the starch is broken down by biological agents. As the starch disappears, so does a large component of the bag's structure, and the bag simply falls apart.

This is where the confusion comes in. Eventually, the removal of all the starch will cause the original plastic bag to disappear in form. However, because it is the starch and not the plastic that has been degraded, *all* the original plastic is still there, it just doesn't look like a plastic bag any more. In fact, the residue can be more damaging than the original bag, since in its essentially powdered form it can be leached into the ground and could eventually contaminate a water supply.

There is a significant downside to "degradable" plastic: it diverts attention away from the real environmental problem, which is the application of energy, water and, in most cases, a non-renewable natural resource to produce a product that has an extremely short lifespan. A better solution is to reduce the amount of plastic being used and thrown away. From the point of view of the manufacturer, however, "degradable" plastics are a way to be seen to address the public's expressed concerns without losing market position. The truth is, though, that "degradable" plastic has little to offer in the way of protecting our natural environment.

Using Plastics Wisely

The explosion in the number of plastics and their applications has definitely made some positive contributions to our standard of living. It can be easily argued that, since they are derived from products extracted for other purposes, plastics represent a more efficient use of those resources. In many applications, they do take pressure off some of our finite resources. The problem is not so much with plastic itself as with the irresponsible manner in which we use the products and with the frivolous consumption of plastics. Remember, there is always an alternative to plastic – something that is not true of most other materials.

Waste Not, Want Not

In older, simpler times, garbage collection was simply a matter of throwing refuse from someone's trash cans into the back of a truck. The collected waste was then driven to an incinerator or landfill site for disposal. Now there is more waste, but fewer landfill spaces, and too many outdated incinerators. Today, waste disposal is one of our major urban dilemmas, and waste management is a high-tech business – and a lucrative one for those companies that anticipated the problems with waste disposal and found opportunity in garbage.

What Are We Throwing Away?

Depending on where you live and your level of consumption, you are probably responsible for 400 to 500 kilograms of household waste each year. Assuming that you do not litter, all of this ends up in landfill sites or incinerators. However, the bulk of this material doesn't need to be there.

Paper

The largest single component of household waste is paper, which can make up as much as one-half of the total garbage you produce. As explained in Chapter 4, our wasteful consumption of paper destroys forests and makes it difficult for reforestation programs to keep up. Pulp and paper production is energy-intensive and is the largest source of water pollution in Canada.

Plants and Animals

By weight, about one-fifth of your garbage is waste food products, and 5 to 15%, depending on where you live and the season, is composed of yard waste such as leaves and cut grass. All this organic material (except meat waste) can be composted. Compost can be used on your lawn and garden in place of chemical fertilizers.

Plastic

Plastic can account for up to 10% of your garbage by weight, but a greater proportion by volume. Because it does not degrade readily, it stays in landfill for a long time. It is also difficult to incinerate. Most of the plastic thrown away does not need to be used in the first place (see Chapter 11), so reducing plastic wastes is easily within everyone's grasp.

The Rest

The balance of household garbage is composed of products such as metal, wood, glass, textiles and other materials. The potential for re-use of many of these wastes is high and, again, reductions can very easily be made.

There are other household wastes that don't necessarily end up in landfills or other waste disposal sites. These may not be thought of as wastes in the same sense as your weekly trash can load. They can, however, have even greater effects on the environment. These include the chemical cocktails that are flushed down your drains and into your gutters as a result of activities around the home.

Waste Disposal Options

We have a limited choice of waste disposal options. We can re-use things, or we can bury or burn them.

Recycling

Recycling not only reduces the amount of garbage, it reduces the need to extract or refine virgin resources. Manufacturing some products from recycled material is also cheaper, since less energy is usually required. However, government subsidies, tax breaks and incentives for the use of raw materials often make recycled products more expensive for the consumer. This higher cost, combined with perceived lower quality, makes recycled material less attractive.

At present, less than 2% of Canada's waste is recycled – far below the levels achieved in many other industrialized countries. However, municipal recycling is catching on like wildfire in southern Ontario and is being heavily promoted in other parts of the country. It is seen as a way of enabling all citizens to do their part to solve the crisis of waste disposal. Indeed, recycling programs have gained so much acceptance in some regions that the supply of recycled material far exceeds the demand. The result is mountains of used newspapers in some areas awaiting buyers. Similarly, household hazardous waste days are often so popular that organizers cannot handle the volume of waste being presented for disposal and must turn people away.

Recycling is popular, there's no doubt about that, and there is significant potential for recycling growth in Canada. However, as long as we can recycle certain household wastes, we have little incentive to *reduce* consumption. That is where the real progress will occur. I am not arguing against recycling; such programs should be supported. But they are only part of the solution. We need to reduce the total amount of garbage we are producing, not just put some of it in the recycling bin.

Composting

Composting is within the reach of all homeowners and can significantly reduce the amount of your garbage. It involves creating an environment where bacteria can break down your organic wastes, such as leaves, grass clippings and vegetable scraps. The resulting product can then be used as fertilizer for your lawn or garden.

On a larger scale, communities accumulate a tremendous amount of organic waste when they clear leaves from parks and streets. Composting these materials and using the compost as fertilizers for parks and green space is an option that should be considered by municipalities. Some municipalities have started to collect leaves from homeowners as well.

Incineration

It used to be acceptable to burn waste. Many of the products that end up in incinerators, though, require very high temperatures to burn efficiently. Inefficient burning produces soot and releases a plethora of harmful chemicals into the environment that would be destroyed at higher temperatures. Similarly, the ash left after burning contains high concentrations of heavy metals and chemicals that are not burned. This ash must still be disposed of and often presents greater problems for safe disposal than the original material did. Incineration is also expensive and requires lots of energy.

Incineration does, however, substantially decrease the volume of waste. The heat generated can also be used for alternate purposes. Charlottetown has an incinerator that can accommodate 120 tonnes of waste per day. The energy produced is used to fuel heating and air conditioning for a local hospital.

Landfill

Sanitary landfill is the most common method of waste disposal in Canada. Waste is transported to a dump, where it is compacted and then covered with a layer of earth. Where land is readily available, landfill does not present an immediate problem. In densely populated areas of the country, though, the scarcity of land and the volume of waste make waste disposal a significant challenge. Such is the case in south central and southwestern Ontario, for example. Some municipalities in the region have taken steps to ban corrugated cardboard from their landfills because the material is re-usable and recyclable and takes up a considerable amount of landfill space.

We don't have to look far to see the future of landfill. In the summer of 1988, a barge of garbage from the northeast United States was rejected from port after port as it tried to find a country foolish enough to accept its cargo. Within a few years, New York City's major dump site will become the highest point of land on the eastern seaboard of the United States!

Sanitary landfill presents several problems. It takes up a lot of space, particularly when light, durable materials such as plastics are involved. It attracts scavenging wildlife, from gulls to bears. As material in the landfill decomposes, potentially dangerous gases, such as methane (which also contributes to global warming) are produced. Hazardous chemicals may also be leached from the landfill into local water supplies. However, landfill is also relatively easy and, in most parts of the country, cheap.

A Closer Look at Packaging

Packaging accounts for up to 50% of our solid waste by volume and is one area in which reductions can be made quickly. The costs of the package and the packaging material are passed along to the consumer. Yet we willingly use our hard-earned dollars to buy packages that go straight into the garbage. There is a continual debate over whether plastic, paper, glass or some other packaging material is "best." The appropriateness of the material depends on the use to which it is being put, and, as usual, there are no simple answers. The following suggestions may help you to make those decisions.

1 **Is the package necessary?** This should be the first question. Wrapping a few beans in plastic and displaying them on a foam tray is wasteful. Similarly, wrapping a potato in plastic and selling it as ready for the microwave oven is nonsense. If a product doesn't need a package, buy it without the package.

2 **Compare the lifespan of the product to that of its package**

If the product will be consumed quickly yet the packaging is more permanent and cannot be re-used or recycled, that's a problem. Consider a single-serving yogurt container. For the sake of two or three spoonfuls of product, a plastic container, often with a foil top, is created that will last for decades.

3 **Relate the amount of packaging to the quantity of product**

Generally, the smaller the quantity purchased, the more packaging is required, proportionately. Buying in larger quantities and creating your own single servings in re-usable containers may take more effort but will save you money and create less garbage.

4 Choose simple packaging Packages made of several different types of material are costly to produce and almost impossible to recycle. A perfect example is the drink-size carton of fruit juice. These paper cartons are lined with a thin layer of metal and wrapped in plastic, yet they contain only a few mouthfuls of beverage. This is excessive, and the combination of different materials makes recycling such containers difficult. Try to purchase products in packages made of only one material.

5 Avoid "blister" packages These packages contain their product in a plastic bubble. Often, such packages may be several times the size of the article contained within, and due to the combination of materials that make up the packaging, they cannot be recycled.

CONTACT: Environmentally Sound Packaging Coalition

Starting Your Own Compost Heap

Composting reduces the amount of organic waste going into landfills and allows gardeners to eliminate the use of chemical fertilizers. All you need is air, water and waste.

1 Select your location The spot you choose should be sunny, with good air circulation and room for you to work.

2 Construct your container The easiest way to make a compost bin is to take a large wooden box, barrel or garbage can and remove the bottom. Holes should be drilled in the sides near the top and bottom of the container to facilitate air circulation.

3 What to compost You need two types of "fuel" – wet and dry. Wet compost can include food wastes from your kitchen (but no meat wastes). Dry compost material gives structure to your pile and assists with air circulation. This material can be leaves, grass or garden clippings, straw and nut shells. You can also use smaller amounts of sawdust, eggshells or other dry organic material.

4 **Getting started**
Alternate layers of dry and wet material approximately 6 to 16 centimetres in depth. A thin layer of chemical fertilizer on the bottom of the pile may be helpful in starting the process.

5 **Keep the pile moist**
The decomposition of the organic matter generates heat which, in turn, facilitates the decomposition of the new material added to the pile. This process can only be maintained if the compost is kept moist. If it is too dry, small amounts of water can be added. If it is too wet, more dry material should be added to absorb excess moisture. If your compost pile smells bad, it is likely too wet.

6 **Stoke the pile**
Every few weeks, the compost needs to be mixed by turning it with a shovel or fork. This action mixes materials in different stages of decomposition and speeds the overall process. It should get the compost generating heat as the process is reactivated. If it doesn't, the compost is ready to be used.

7 **Add small pieces**
The composting process will be accelerated if you cut waste into small pieces. Instead of throwing in a whole lemon rind, for example, cut it into slices first.

8 **Cover your compost pile**
In the summer, a cover is necessary to keep the mixture from becoming too wet or dry. In the winter, it keeps the heat that fuels the process from dissipating.

9 **Don't feed the animals**
Your neighbours will appreciate it if your compost heap doesn't smell bad or attract nocturnal visitors. If you are maintaining the right moisture balance, odours shouldn't be a problem. Avoiding the use of meat wastes can prevent visits from cats, dogs, raccoons and skunks. An insect screen can also help to keep flies away.

10 Apartment composting
Due to limited space, composting is difficult for apartment dwellers. But if you keep house plants and have a balcony, you could try experimenting with a scaled-down compost pile.

Reduce Your Waste Production

Reducing waste is relatively easy, but who wants to think about garbage? However, there is no better way to assess your attitude to the natural environment than to take a critical look at what you are putting out at the curb or down the chute each week. You don't have to be a fanatic and try to make your home self-sufficient, but making a significant dent in your waste output won't hurt a bit and will likely save you money.

1 Buy quality and extend the lifespan of all goods
Buy the highest-quality item you can afford. The principle behind cheap products is that once they wear out or break down you will throw them out and buy something new. In the long run, buying quality and then spending money on maintenance and repairs is far more advantageous to your pocketbook and to the environment. Resoling a good pair of shoes, for example, is far less expensive, and more comfortable, than buying a new pair.

2 Avoid "disposables"
Items are truly disposable only if they will eventually degrade into their natural components. Even if those conditions are met, it is not always appropriate to favour disposable items over re-usable ones. Products to avoid include disposable diapers (which also present a sewage disposal problem), razors, cameras and just about anything made of plastic.

3 Avoid packaging
A large part of the paper and plastic found in garbage is packaging for food and other household products. Avoid

this by buying in bulk wherever possible. You will also save money by not paying for those packages that you throw in the garbage!

4 **Use recyclable containers**
Select bottles that are identified as refillable and return them once used. If there is a recycling program or depot in your community for non-refillable bottles or cans, support it. Similarly, if a plastic recycling program is available, some plastic bottles may be acceptable. However, refillable glass bottles should be your container of choice.

5 **Donate**
Hospitals or doctors' offices may welcome used books or magazines for their waiting rooms. Old clothing and furniture can be given to Goodwill or the Salvation Army's thrift shops. Unusually shaped bottles may be of interest to stores that sell home-brewing supplies. Used books might find a home with a bookseller, or a local library, if they are in good condition. Be creative.

6 **Profit from your waste**
The Great Canadian Waste Exchange is the garage sale. In some parts of the country, garage sales are a cottage industry. If you don't feel you have enough unwanted material for a sale, pool efforts with a neighbour or two. These events are popular partly for their social aspect, and partly for what people learn about their neighbours. Tabloid newspapers long ago discovered that you can learn a lot about people by poking through their trash!

7 **One person's waste is another's raw material**
Much of the material finding its way into our garbage is not only recyclable, it is valuable! Used appliances, furniture, metal and other items may be of interest to scrap dealers, who will pay you for them.

8 **Compost**
A large part of your household waste is organic material, such as vegetable scraps and garden waste, which can be easily composted into fertilizer for your garden, or for a neighbour's if you are not a gardener. Composting is one activity that can lead to an

immediate reduction in the amount of waste you discard. At the same time, by using a more natural fertilizer, you are reducing the unnecessary use of chemicals.

Hazardous Waste Disposal

One of the hypocrisies that we bring to environmental issues is our attitude toward hazardous wastes. Communities welcome industries that can provide needed jobs and economic growth. The plants themselves may contribute to the despoliation of the natural environment in the region, but the trade-off and risks are deemed worthwhile. What is usually not accepted, though, is the storage or disposal of the hazardous chemicals that may be generated by the industry.

Your local hazardous waste site can be a pretty unhealthy place. The chemicals that are stored there are in high concentration, and most are known to be dangerous to the environment and/or human health. Even a small leak from a container can do damage. To make matters worse, there are numerous hazardous waste sites around the country whose ownership cannot be determined. In Nova Scotia alone, a recent survey found 172 abandoned hazardous waste sites. Citizens can demand that a major corporation clean up its act, but if you can't identify who is responsible or hold them accountable, then that is impossible. These so-called "orphan" sites also pose a significant risk because it is not always possible to identify what is stored there.

We should, of course, strive to reduce hazardous waste, but disposal is a problem that will always be with us. Therefore, as a society, we had better face up to our responsibilities. That means taking care of the waste we create. Environmentally sound disposal facilities are expensive and require skilled operators. It is unreasonable to believe that every community will be able to provide the service. However, centralized disposal within provinces or regions, or mobile disposal facilities, could do the job. This would reduce the need for transportation of hazardous wastes, which is the riskiest phase of disposal.

Storage or disposal sites for hazardous wastes are understandably unpopular with people who live nearby. If properly established and operated, however, they pose no more risk than many of the industries that produced the waste in the first place. Again, the problem is attitude: a pulp mill or a refinery is "good" because it provides jobs and produces goods that we value; a hazardous waste disposal site is "bad" even though its environmental risks may be no greater.

CONTACT: Pollution Probe

The Future of Waste

The population of this planet is growing. Every new person stretches the earth's resources a little bit farther and generates waste that must be disposed of. Our major cities are microcosms of what the outcome of this may be. The high concentration of people produces a large amount of waste. Because land is valued for settlement, and people are concerned about their air, water and health, not to mention aesthetics, waste disposal sites become hard to find. Those that do exist are bursting at the seams.

We must change our attitude to garbage. Waste is one of the best sources of raw materials, since much of what is thrown away is reusable. Cutting down on waste will make every home more efficient and will save resources. Recovering materials through recycling or reuse will also take pressure off both our waste disposal systems and our natural resources.

The answer to the waste problem is fairly simple: use only what you need and use it efficiently. Despite the benefits to people's pocketbooks and to the planet, it seems to be a difficult concept to get across!

13

Environmental Protection in the Workplace

Now that your home is a more environmentally friendly place, let's look at your workplace, assuming you don't work at home. Where you are in the hierarchy of the organization, and the amount of direct control you have over corporate decisions, will influence your effectiveness at work. However, no matter what your position, a variety of options are within your reach, as an individual and in conjunction with co-workers. Your actions may even eventually pervade the entire company, particularly if they contribute to the morale or productivity of employees.

The important thing to remember in advancing your environmental concerns is that environmental protection is in everybody's best interests. It's just that many individuals and businesses don't know it yet! Often the reasons presented for not adopting environmentally friendly techniques and practices are convenient excuses for ignoring the issues and hoping they will go away. They won't. The businesses that recognize the opportunity inherent in incorporating environmental protection into their operations will realize a healthier and more productive workforce and a more efficient operation. Higher profits will follow.

Now all you have to do is convince your employer.

Corporate Leadership

We bemoan the fact that industrial activities despoil the environment. Yet we ignore the fact that when many plants or procedures were developed the *public* demonstrated very little concern for the environment. Industries prosper because we buy their products or services, implicitly endorsing their methods. And as shareholders, we get upset if companies are unprofitable and don't pay dividends.

As we become more aware and vocal about environmental matters, many industries are responding by cleaning up their act. New procedures are being developed to reduce the pollution caused by industrial processes. Most industries, just like most people, will modify their behaviour as a result of incentives rather than penalties. Certainly, it is a more positive and enjoyable way of achieving progress.

Developing a corporate environmental ethic can be a winning proposition at all levels of the organization, no matter what the business. Everybody likes to be part of a positive effort, and if co-workers are all participating, the sense of solidarity and that old standby, peer pressure, help to sustain the effort. Businesses can take advantage of these opportunities with remarkably little effort.

I'll always remember my first meeting with Murray Chercover, CEO of the CTV television network. He took me on a tour of CTV's offices, gleefully showing off the paper recycling bins located throughout. Similarly, senior executives of General Foods glowed about one of their plants that had managed to attract Canada geese to a pond on the property. To see the enthusiasm with which many people embrace such positive steps for the environment only makes you wonder why we allow so many of our destructive practices to continue!

Corporations become involved in environmental issues for a variety of reasons. Some experience direct business benefits, while others benefit only indirectly or not at all. There are a lot of corporations that want to buy an environmental image the way they purchase any other commodity. Far fewer are demonstrating their concern through action, but those that do receive a multitude of benefits, through both increased profitability and an improved public profile. In addition to becoming environmentally responsible in all aspects of their operations, all businesses have the potential to provide leadership on environmental issues in their communities. The motivation is not important. Action is.

Two Corporate Examples

The Fort Whyte Centre for Environmental Education

In the 1960s, an employee of Canada Cement Lafarge in Winnipeg began attracting waterfowl to the human-made lakes that provide the cement plant with water. He convinced his employer to set aside the land surrounding the lakes as a sanctuary. Over several years, Canada Cement Lafarge performed a number of land swaps to allow the sanctuary to grow. Local service clubs and foundations funded the sanctuary, and good educational programs were established, largely through the efforts of volunteers. Today, the Fort Whyte Centre for Environmental Education is one of the premier interpretive facilities in the country. It operates in the shadow of Canada Cement Lafarge's kilns, and its lakes still provide the plant's water supply.

Ahead of Its Time

Mohawk Oil was the recipient of Canada's first Environmental Achievement Award for Corporations, presented by Environment Canada in 1989. Mohawk developed and implemented a recycling program for oil products more than a decade ago, well before environmental protection achieved its current prominence. And it has made the program profitable. At the same time, Mohawk is producing gasohol, a combination of gasoline and ethanol, which is cleaner-burning than regular gasoline. Mohawk proves that there is profit in environmental protection.

The Environmentally Friendly Workplace

All the recommendations in this book regarding the home can be applied just as well to the workplace. There are, however, some things that are more common at work. The following actions can be initiated by individual employees, unions or management.

1 **Purchase wisely**
Buy locally and support businesses that have good environmental records. Purchase only what your business really needs, and buy quality. Purchase goods made from recycled material whenever possible.

2 **Establish sound maintenance practices**
Get the maximum life out of your building and equipment. Regular maintenance can extend their useful life and reduce the need for application of raw materials.

3 **Create an environmentally friendly staff room**
Lessen dependence on fast food outlets and the waste associated with them by providing a sink, a refrigerator and equipment for cooking and making coffee. Get rid of disposable cups, cutlery and stir sticks in favour of re-usable items. Stock milk, sugar and condiments in bulk to eliminate the need for single-serving packages. To encourage employees to eat in, provide social or recreational activities during meal breaks.

4 **Don't forget the bathroom**
Use cloth towels instead of paper or air dryers for hands. Purchase recycled toilet paper. Use refillable liquid soap containers.

5 **Reduce water use**
It is likely that in every activity, from the manufacturing process to the maintenance of buildings and grounds to the staff room, more water is used in each application than is really necessary.

6 **Cut down on paper use**
Computers were supposed to lessen our reliance on paper, but the reverse is happening. Before printing out something, or distributing memos and other correspondence, question the need for the document and don't make any more copies than are absolutely necessary. Don't go fax-crazy – fax paper can't be recycled.

7 Get the maximum mileage out of paper

Office paper can be re-used as scratch paper, replacing the need for pads. It can also be cut up for use as notepaper and memo pads. Use a photocopier that is capable of two-sided copying.

8 Set up a paper recycling program

Once paper has been fully used, it can be collected in bins and sent for recycling. Contact local recycling agencies to find one that can serve your workplace.

9 Cut down on couriers

Much of what is sent by courier is not urgent enough to warrant the service. Paying someone to deliver a package by bicycle or on foot is okay, but automobile deliveries contribute to environmental problems and should only be used when absolutely necessary.

10 Cut down on air travel

See if business can be conducted by telephone, computer or fax before planning a business trip. Send packages by air freight only when they are urgently required at their destination. Otherwise favour rail or truck transport.

11 Operate fuel-efficient fleets

If your business maintains vehicles on the road, use the most fuel-efficient ones possible and convert them to cleaner-burning fuels, such as propane or natural gas.

12 Support public transit

Most employers, particularly those who own the land on which they operate, provide free parking for their employees, encouraging the use of automobiles. Similar subsidies are rarely provided to employees who use public transit. Either charge for parking or subsidize transit fares.

13 Make your building energy efficient

The rules that apply to home heating and cooling (see Chapter 2) also relate to businesses. If your business involves a manufacturing process that generates heat, it may be possible to use the energy produced to heat and cool plant buildings.

14 Use light efficiently

One of the standard problems assigned to business school students is to evaluate the efficiency of changing light bulbs in an office building. Conventional wisdom holds that the most efficient method is to replace them all at regular intervals, regardless of whether they are burned out or not. However, that is the case only if labour is the sole factor considered. From an environmental perspective, you should be using the most economical light source possible and replacing bulbs only when they burn out.

15 Turn off lights and equipment

When items are not in use, turn them off. Buildings with all the lights on at night burn a lot of energy, not to mention bulbs. Brightly lit windows are also a magnet for birds, which are often injured or killed by colliding with the glass.

16 Avoid open freezers

Open freezers and coolers waste energy. Frequent opening and closing of doors affects the efficiency of a closed unit, but this is only a problem during office hours, and closed units have a greater overall efficiency.

17 Landscape for nature

The grounds around your building can be landscaped to complement the natural environment. Not only will this beautify surroundings, it can attract wildlife.

18 Cut down on chemicals

It is possible to eliminate or reduce the use of many chemicals around the workplace. For example, printers may be able to switch from organic-based inks to water-based ones. This applies to maintenance as well as the manufacturing process. Look for less damaging alternatives wherever possible (see Chapter 10).

19 Recover wastes wherever possible

Recovery of wastes cuts down on the need for raw materials and can improve the profitability of any business, whether it is a steel mill, film processor, dry-cleaner or car wash.

20 Recycle construction materials

If your business involves construction, use recycled material in the preparation of products, and recycle used material such as glass, metal, asphalt, concrete and rubber.

21 Participate in waste exchanges

What is waste in some manufacturing processes is necessary in others. Many provinces have exchanges where waste materials can be bought and sold, thus reducing the amount that must be disposed of and keeping everyone's costs down.

22 Dispose of waste appropriately

All businesses should be encouraging employees to cut down the amount of garbage generated in daily operations. Similarly, employers should be looking for examples of waste in their manufacturing or distribution processes and eliminating them.

23 Above all, practise self-criticism

Everything from the organization's daily activities to its corporate policies should be regularly reviewed to ensure that waste is reduced, resources are used wisely, and the corporation is a good environmental citizen.

Profit from Environmental Protection

Pollution Probe, one of Canada's foremost environmental organizations, has produced a book called *Profit from Pollution Prevention.* Information is provided to enable most manufacturers to eliminate harmful or wasteful practices, recover and re-use wastes and reduce the amount of contaminants or waste produced in the operation. The book is available at a cost of $25 from Pollution Probe, 12 Madison Avenue, Toronto, Ontario, M5R 2S1.

Hazardous Chemicals and Wastes

Many businesses, particularly those in the manufacturing sector, produce wastes that can be classified as hazardous and use hazardous chemicals in their operations. The following is a checklist to consider in handling these products.

1 **Are the hazardous chemicals in use necessary?** Are new processes available that could lessen the requirement for hazardous chemicals? In the case of cleaners or solvents, are they really necessary or simply used for convenience?

2 **Are chemicals used in the right concentrations?** To reduce waste and the possibility of contamination, the minimum amount of chemicals should be applied to achieve the desired result, and they should be applied as efficiently as possible.

3 **What effort is made to recover and re-use waste chemicals?** Re-using chemicals will reduce the amount of waste that must be disposed of. Since this practice is likely to be more efficient, it could save the business money in the long run.

4 **How is the material stored and catalogued?** Does the company store hazardous chemicals in a secure place, or are they located where virtually anyone has access to them? Are the amounts used recorded and checked against inventories?

5 **Are workers properly trained in the use of the materials?** Many chemical spills and accidents are caused by employees who are unfamiliar with the properties of the material they are handling. If a company expects workers to use the chemical, it has an obligation to train them in the safest method of doing so.

6 **Is protective equipment supplied?** The safe use of hazardous chemicals and wastes requires the provision of appropriate protective clothing and equipment.

7 Does the company have emergency plans for a spill, leak or fire?
All companies using hazardous chemicals or generating toxic wastes should have contingency plans in readiness should an accident occur.

8 How are unwanted wastes disposed of?
Does your company deal with a professional waste disposal contractor who can ensure that unwanted hazardous chemicals are disposed of in a safe and environmentally responsible manner? If wastes are destroyed on site, is this done in the safest manner possible?

Facing the Future

Rightly or not, business has become the villain of the environmental war. There is an annoying tendency among some members of the environmental movement to tar all industries and companies with the same brush: anything done to create profits is automatically "bad," and intentions are not "honourable" no matter how much benefit accrues to the environment in the process. This attitude creates an obstacle to those companies trying to demonstrate environmental leadership.

The business world doesn't operate today the same way it did one hundred years ago, or even twenty years ago. It is constantly changing in response to the demands of its customers and society in general. There is every reason to believe that the process will continue and that an environmental ethic, *if cultivated properly*, will become an essential component of good business practice.

We are fond of noting that concern for the environment is higher than ever, and that it is one of the top issues of concern to Canadians of all backgrounds. Since the majority of these people work for a living, it is not inconceivable that this concern will start to pervade the workplace. From the shop floor to the boardroom, the workplace is people, and sooner or later their concerns are going to influence the way every business operates.

Some businesses will respond positively and take initiatives to protect the environment. Others will move only after they see the front-runners succeeding. Still others may have to be prodded into it through legislation or the loss of sales. But if the concern keeps up, change will occur. The actions of employees can be a major contributor to this process.

Environmentally Friendly Communities

For years, the maxim that has guided the environmental movement has been "Think globally, act locally." Solving environmental problems is not going to be a "top-down" process. Environmental protection begins at home. The cumulative actions of 26 million Canadians will not only contribute significantly to the health of the Canadian environment, they will send a clear signal to business and government that the old ways are no longer acceptable. If the people who vote and pay the bills demonstrate environmentally responsible behaviour, the national and global solutions will fall into place – an environmental equivalent to "Look after the pennies, and the dollars will look after themselves."

Closer to home politically, the influence of a city or town council over the environment is considerable. Municipal governments, depending on the size of the community, may have jurisdiction directly or through contractors over sewage treatment, water supply, public transit, zoning, garbage collection and disposal, weed control, animal control, utilities, road construction and maintenance and green space. In terms of activities that directly affect the environment, your municipal government is at the forefront. It therefore carries a tremendous environmental responsibility.

Evaluating Municipal Performance

To assess the capabilities and performance of your municipal government on environmental issues, you must examine a broad range of topics. Each one has a profound impact on the natural environment and on the quality of life within the community.

▪ ***How is water protected?***
Where does your water supply come from and what measures are taken to ensure its safety? Is water use metered? Are prices for water high enough to encourage people to conserve it? Is water rationing imposed when necessary? How are the industries or communities that discharge waste into your community's drinking water supply regulated? If your community is on a river, lake or ocean, are steps being taken to restrict shoreline development to prevent erosion and loss of habitat?

▪ ***How does your sewage treatment stack up?***
Slightly more than half of Canadian communities treat their sewage. The balance discharge their waste untreated into a water supply. Many existing sewage treatment facilities are aging and are not designed to remove the types of chemicals that we now know are found in our sewage. Unless your community has a separate system for storm run-off, heavy rains or thaws can disrupt normal sewage treatment procedures, releasing raw sewage into the environment.

What sort of sewage treatment exists in your community? If sewage isn't treated, what plans are in place to provide the service? If you do have a treatment facility, what is its lifespan and capabilities? Are there plans to upgrade?

▪ ***What type of waste disposal system is available?***
Does your community use landfill or incineration? Are the rates charged for waste disposal subsidized? Cheap disposal costs do not encourage industries that use municipal waste sites to cut down on their garbage. What is the lifespan of your community's waste disposal facility? What plans are in place to augment or replace it? Are there any hazardous waste dumps within your community? How are they policed?

▪ ***How is waste managed?***
Garbage collection is performed either by municipal employees or by a private contractor. Sometimes both exist within one community. Are recycling programs in place in your community? What plans exist to start or expand recycling programs? Does the municipal government have its own internal recycling programs? Does your municipal-

ity encourage composting? Does it compost its own organic waste? What provision does your community make for centralized disposal of hazardous wastes?

- ***What type of energy is being supported?***

If your community owns its own utility company, what form of energy does it favour? If it is thermal power, what type of fuel is burned? Are municipal buildings heated and cooled in an environmentally compatible manner? Does the municipal government have an energy conservation program? Do municipal vehicles use gasoline, diesel, propane or natural gas as fuel?

- ***How are your roads maintained?***

An incredible amount of sand and salt is placed on municipal streets every winter. Often, it can actually make driving conditions worse. It is certainly not good for either cars or the road. Most of it is blown onto lawns and roadsides immediately after application, and all of it eventually ends up in the local water supply. What sort of road maintenance is practised in your community? Are alternatives being explored?

Construction and repair of roads is also a municipal responsibility. Does your community encourage the use of recycled material in road construction?

- ***What sort of transportation is encouraged?***

Does your community provide bicycle paths or lanes? Has the municipal government ever considered assessing tolls or restricting the number of occupants per car on certain routes? Are city centres and business districts designed to be friendly to pedestrians, or do they encourage automobiles?

- ***Do you have an effective public transit system?***

The provision of public transit is generally a municipal responsibility and will, of course, depend on the size and geographic layout of the community. What systems are available in your community? Are fares subsidized to encourage use? Is your community's development oriented to transit corridors? Are bus lanes provided on roads during rush hours? What plans are in place to expand or enhance your community's system?

▪ ***Does zoning favour the environment?***
Developers tend to carry considerable weight at city hall. To these people, a vacant lot or green space is seen as a development waiting to be approved. Urban sprawl destroys a substantial amount of agricultural land and wildlife habitat each year. Expanding communities also encourage road extensions and discourage public transit. Is your community expansionist, or does it develop according to a plan that allows for a quality urban environment with efficient delivery of services and consideration for the surrounding landscape?

▪ ***What value is placed on green space?***
Livable cities and towns provide for a lot of green space. Ottawa and Edmonton are good examples. Without green space, such as parks, cities become sterile environments with little life except people and pigeons. What value does your municipal government place on green space? (Golf courses don't count.)

▪ ***Does your community use drugs?***
Roadsides and parks are treated chemically to attempt to control weeds and insects. In some areas, aerial spraying is also conducted, indiscriminately dumping tonnes of chemicals on a community. What types of chemicals are being introduced into your local environment? Has your community explored alternatives such as natural pest control?

▪ ***Does your community provide humane and effective animal control?***
Animal feces in the urban environment are a significant health hazard to humans, and stray pets create a variety of problems for humans, other animals and themselves. Effective laws governing household pets actually benefit pets and pet owners. Does your community operate an archaic "catch-and-release" program for dogs, or does it offer pro-active and effective animal control programs that seek to prevent animal problems? Who is responsible for handling problem wildlife in your community? Do they address problems by killing wildlife, or by focusing on prevention and the relocation of problem animals?

If you don't usually give much thought to municipal politics, perhaps this will change your mind: *no* level of government can have as much direct influence on the environment as the municipal government. It is up to you, as a citizen of the community, to ensure that your municipal government is exercising the full powers available to it to protect the local environment and, most important, is aware of the leadership role that it must take in this area.

Community Organizing

Whatever your goal, whether supporting the development of a recycling program or opposing a development that will destroy wildlife habitat, it is unlikely that you will be able to attain it alone. Nor should you. If the issue is going to affect others in your community, then all those people should participate in the resolution of the problem. Your task is to find a core group of fellow activists, plan strategy, coordinate everyone's efforts and then communicate your concerns effectively.

1 **Be a "green" volunteer** Many community organizations address environmental issues, and they all rely extensively on volunteer support. The easiest way to play a role in making your community more friendly to the environment is to get involved with one of these groups. They will appreciate your help.

2 **Don't reinvent the wheel** If you are concerned about a specific problem, start by contacting established local groups in your area. Too often, when individuals take on an environmental problem, they are unaware of, or even ignore, the efforts of others and attempt to start their own campaign. There may already be an environmental group, citizens' committee, church or social group, or some other body working on or addressing matters related to your issue of concern.

Do some homework. Ask people you know in your community, municipal employees, the media and individuals or businesses involved if they can direct you to an existing group. If you find one, learn what they have done and what they plan to do. Talk to their board of directors and members of their executive. If they are working on the issue, volunteer to help them. If they aren't working on the issue but it is related to other campaigns or concerns they may have, see if you can get some support from them in organizing your campaign.

3 **Don't burn bridges** If you cannot persuade an existing group to get involved in your issue, don't go away mad. Understand that everyone who takes up a torch for an issue feels that theirs is the most important concern of the day. If a group, or some of its members, has different priorities, that does not mean that your issue is not important or that the group is not interested. Virtually all community groups have limited resources and cannot overextend themselves without diluting their effectiveness. Strive to maintain good relations with all the groups operating in your sphere of interest, and you will be surprised how much valuable support and advice they may give you, whether or not they choose to become actively involved in your cause.

4 **Find your core members** One of the easiest ways to find members is to secure a location for a public meeting, even if it is your basement, and place a notice in your local community newspaper. Arrange to have someone knowledgeable on the issue make a brief presentation to the audience, and ask those interested to sign a register. You can then schedule a follow-up meeting at a later date and invite those who registered to attend.

5 **Get experts on your side** Unless you can turn out a significant number of citizens to a municipal government meeting, you are going to have to win your campaign with facts (and even that doesn't always work!). If there is a university or community college in your community, see if anyone on the faculty has particular expertise relating to your issue. If not, perhaps some knowledgeable people in the private sector might be willing to volunteer their services. Lawyers, accountants, public relations profession-

als and others can also offer valuable advice regarding your campaign. And if you can convince one or two prominent citizens to endorse your efforts, doors will open rapidly.

6 Don't ignore the decision makers

Cultivate good relationships with bureaucrats and municipal politicians. If you dismiss or distrust all the people with whom you must deal, issues will frequently degenerate into a polarized campaign for public or political support. By developing good relationships, you will make life a lot easier for yourself. Securing the support of a prominent municipal politician can provide you with a wealth of advice on lobbying. You'd also be surprised how open bureaucrats can be with information and advice that you wouldn't otherwise have access to.

7 Research

Sounds simple, doesn't it? However, many activists find their campaigns short-circuited when they are placed in situations where their knowledge of the facts is tested. Always assume that your opposition knows more than you do. Learn everything you can about the issue. Your research will help you identify experts who may be able to offer further assistance. If you are going to cite examples and/or statistics in your campaign, make sure that they are relevant or applicable to your community. Your credibility will hinge on getting the right information and using it correctly.

8 Network

Seek the advice of successful advocacy groups, even if their issues are unrelated to yours. If you have made good contacts with local community or environmental groups, they may be able to refer you to people in other communities who are fighting, or who have fought, similar campaigns. Contact them and learn from their successes and failures.

9 Communicate

Talk to as many people as possible about your concern. Try especially to get the media to cover your cause. The easiest way to do this is to issue a press release. Present your arguments in a balanced format, explaining why the matter is important to your community and its citizens. Remember to adhere to the KISS (keep it simple, stupid) principle. Avoid emotion and rhetoric as much as possible and, in all of your public messages, keep personalities out of the debate. Focus on the issue and the facts and avoid confrontations unless they are strategically appropriate (see below) or there is no alternative.

10 Praise

Virtually all politicians thrive on public attention, and they would all prefer it to be positive rather than negative! Environmentalists are often perceived as a rather dour lot who never have a good thing to say about anyone or anything. Even when they grudgingly give praise, it is tempered by the suggestion that the government's actions are welcome but insufficient. That may be true, but you don't train a dog by kicking it. Praise and giving credit where credit is due are effective advocacy tools, yet they tend to be used the least.

11 Use confrontation strategically

Picket lines and protests regularly make the news, and certainly give the participants a sense that they are doing something. But their effectiveness depends on the circumstances. Berating politicians does have its place. But if it is the only weapon in your arsenal, you don't have much of a case. Such tactics should only be one component of your campaign and should be used sparingly. If the issue is truly for the benefit of the community, and provides political or economic opportunity, smart politicians will respond readily. Nothing symbolizes a lost cause better than dwindling numbers of protesters being ignored by virtually everyone.

12 Persist

Quick decisions by governments are made only in times of crisis, or when there is an immediate opportunity. Depending on your issue, you might have to work for years to persuade your municipal government to do what you and your group want. Burnout is common among activists, and governments know that the longer they stall on an unpopular issue (and they have an infinite number of ways of doing so) and the more hoops they make you jump through, the more likely you are to go away. It will be necessary for you to go through the same arguments over and over again. But stick it out!

The NIMBY Syndrome

We are all in favour of waste disposal facilities, yet none of us wants to live near one. "Not In My Back Yard!" we cry, thereby giving a name – NIMBY – to the syndrome. It also applies to choosing sites for certain industries, such as nuclear power plants.

Given concerns about existing waste disposal sites, it is understandable that people don't want a new one near their homes. New technologies, though, render many new waste disposal sites no more harmful than the industries that created the wastes in the first place. It is hypocritical, for instance, to welcome a new pulp mill or refinery because of the jobs it provides, while arguing against a waste disposal site.

Granted, people have a right to be concerned about the risks of certain industries near their homes. Most will agree that those industries or waste disposal sites are necessary, but few will voluntarily bite the bullet and welcome them. In the battle to see who can yell the loudest or wield the most political clout, the spoils go to the loser. But the real risk with products such as hazardous wastes is in transport; and the further away from their point of creation they must go, the higher the risk.

For some people, even a minuscule risk is too much, but that argument can be used against almost any form of development. Determining an acceptable level of risk is the root of the problem. If we want the benefits of technology, we must accept the disadvantages as well and address them responsibly.

Moving Communities into the Future

Cities, with their high concentration of people and enormous demand for services, place great pressures on the local environment. Our urban centres were not designed with environmental protection in mind. Any improvements to municipal practices, particularly those that involve capital outlays, are going to carry a price tag, and these costs are going to be passed on to the consumer in the form of increased property taxes. We keep saying that we are willing to pay more for environmental protection, but municipal politicians will be understandably reluctant to make the tough decisions necessary to improve environmental performance unless they are convinced of public support. Are you willing to put your money where your mouth is?

15

Acting Beyond Your Community

Your actions and those of your community can accomplish only so much. To have an effect on the broader environmental issues, you need to work with others who share your concerns, and you will need to target industry leaders and politicians at the provincial, territorial and federal levels. Granted, the farther you go up the line, the bigger the problem you will likely be addressing and the less impact that you, relatively, can have on issues. Politicians rarely lead, however, and certainly in recent years they have become followers of public opinion. Business also responds to the demands of its customers. The more public support shown for environmental protection, the more action that can be squeezed out of governments and industries.

The Warning Signs

Canada's endangered species are sending us a warning about our failure to manage our environmental responsibilities properly. The Committee on the Status of Endangered Wildlife in Canada (COSEWIC) is a joint project of federal, provincial and territorial governments and major conservation organizations. It evaluates the status of species of Canadian wildlife that are believed to be facing threat of extinction and categorizes them according to the degree of threat: vulnerable, threatened and endangered, in order of increasing danger.

Since 1986, the list of such species has almost doubled in size, to 180 species. During that time, only one species, the white pelican, has been removed from the list, and one more, the wood bison, was downgraded in status. As COSEWIC doesn't consider invertebrates and does not have sufficient funds to evaluate all species, the number in danger is likely much higher.

Although extinctions are perfectly natural, the actions of humans are contributing to a much higher rate of species extinctions worldwide than would otherwise be experienced. All species have a role to play within natural ecosystems. The loss of a species may have ramifications for whole systems. From a purely selfish perspective, many species have provided medicinal benefits to humans leading to the development of some essential drugs. Curare is one example. However, many species, particularly in tropical regions, are disappearing before their potential benefits can be assessed.

Nothing symbolizes the state of Canada's environment better than the growing number of species in danger.

CONTACT: World Wildlife Fund (Canada)
Canadian Nature Federation

How Is Your Environment Being Managed?

All of the practical suggestions in this book also have a political message. Here are a few of the things to consider in assessing the manner in which your resources and the environment are being treated. Natural resource and environmental issues are invariably complex, so this list is by no means comprehensive.

- ***Does talk coincide with action?*** Our federal government is making a lot of noise about global warming and atmospheric pollution, yet it continues to provide huge subsidies for the development of new oil and gas reserves which will contribute to these very problems. Is your government really serious about environmental protection, or is it business as usual with a "green" face?

- ***Does your province or territory have a conservation strategy?*** Many jurisdictions are developing conservation strategies to serve as the basis for land-use and resource management decisions. However, only Prince Edward Island has completed its strategy to date. An overall strategy, supported by industry and the public, encourages environmental protection and the wise use of resources.

▪ ***Are you giving your resources away?***
Canada is a major exporter of energy, forest products, metals and minerals and food. Lately, in a number of cases governments have entered into long-term arrangements to provide electricity, coal or pulp at a low price to other countries. It is hypocritical for Canadians to promote a responsible attitude toward consumption domestically while supporting the wasteful practices of other countries.

▪ ***Is environmental destruction being subsidized?***
Different government departments often have different objectives for the same piece of land. For example, a wildlife department may be trying to persuade farmers to maintain potholes and marginal lands for wildlife while an agriculture department may be encouraging the development of these same areas for farming.

Governments may also provide subsidies and incentives to industry to develop new resources. Recycling programs and conservation measures rarely benefit from the same incentives. Is your government sending wrong or conflicting messages through financial subsidies?

▪ ***Are all natural resource developments subject to environmental assessments?***
The potential environmental implications of all activities should be assessed *before* the decision is made to proceed. Too often, studies are done after the fact and look only at how to minimize the impact of a project. We also tend to evaluate the effects of a number of projects in the same area on an individual, rather than a cumulative, basis. How does your government assess developments? Does the public have full input into decisions?

▪ ***How is industry encouraged to protect the environment?***
At each of the different levels of government in Canada, there is a multitude of environmental legislation. Much of it overlaps, standards vary and there are some gaps. Does your government have comprehensive environmental legislation? Does existing legislation have teeth, and is it enforced aggressively? Has your government considered incentive programs to encourage industry to improve, or does it rely solely on legislation?

▪ ***How are hazardous wastes managed?***
What options are available for reducing, storing and disposing of hazardous wastes in your region? Is your government exploring alternatives? How are waste disposal sites regulated? What provisions are made for cleaning up "orphan" sites?

▪ ***What priority does water have?***
How high a priority does your government place on ensuring that all citizens within your region benefit from clean, fresh water? Are plans in place to clean up rivers, lakes and shorelines? How close are industries in your area to achieving "zero discharge?"

▪ ***What energy policy is followed?***
Does your province or territory favour hydroelectricity, coal-fired thermal electricity, nuclear energy, natural gas or oil? How aggressively does it encourage energy conservation? What sort of support does it provide for research into new sources of energy?

▪ ***Do your forests have a future?***
How are timber quotas set? Is overcutting allowed during times of high demand? What types of reforestation programs are in place? Is there a good climate of co-operation between industry and government over reforestation? What percentage of the lands cut annually are reforested, and how successful is reforestation? How is the application of pesticides and herbicides controlled? Are governments and industries considering alternatives? What is the policy on fire control?

▪ ***How are non-renewable resources managed?***
Are all lands in your province or territory open to mineral exploration? What environmental controls are placed on mine sites and smelters to reduce air and water pollution? Are there plans in place to upgrade environmental protection at mines and smelters in your region?

▪ ***Does wildlife conservation extend to all species?***
Most wildlife departments concentrate their efforts on only a few species of wildlife – primarily those that are hunted, fished or trapped. Of the 183

species considered vulnerable, threatened or endangered in Canada, only a few fit this category. How much effort does your wildlife department expend on non-game species, endangered species and assisting people interested in wildlife viewing?

- ***What is your government's policy on protected areas?***

Is your government committed to completing an adequate network of protected areas? Is mineral exploration, timber cutting, hunting or commercial development allowed in parks and protected areas? Demand that your government set aside parks and protected areas that are undisturbed by these activities.

- ***Are governments and industries setting an example?***

Do governments and industries in your region have in-house recycling or waste reduction programs? Are their vehicles fuel efficient? Do they use clean-burning fuels? Are energy conservation programs in place for government buildings and vehicles?

Obviously, you alone cannot assess many of these issues. Fortunately, though, many organizations exist to do this on your behalf. Environmental groups act as watchdogs over governments and industries, and many work constructively with government and industry to develop effective solutions to environmental problems.

Getting Involved

The media attention focused on environmental matters could easily lead one to believe that hundreds of problems are about to blow up in our faces. Many problems are, but the important ones are not necessarily the ones that make the news. One of the toughest tasks for the concerned citizen is deciding which of the multitude of environmental problems, many of which are described in this book, are priorities.

Once you have determined which issue concerns you the most, you can become involved in the decision-making process in a variety of ways. Individually, you can become your own environmental watchdog by writing politicians on issues of concern to you. You can also participate in environmental organizations at the provincial and national levels.

- ***Go beyond the headlines***

Environmental issues are far too complex to be effectively covered in headlines or short news segments. Flesh out your knowledge by reading newsmagazines and books on the subject, and try to find several sources of information.

- ***Contact the experts***

You can contact technical experts in universities, industry, governments or environmental organizations to obtain more in-depth information on issues of concern to you. Each of these will have their own perspective, so try to find several sources of information and consider all the arguments.

- ***Vote for environmentally aware politicians***

Since virtually all politicians say they support environmental protection, words alone do not indicate commitment. But if candidates can talk intelligently about environmental issues, the potential for action exists. Try to go beyond their rhetoric. For example, how does the politician's stand on the economy or regional development mesh with the one he or she has taken on the environment?

- ***Educate politicians***

Once environmentally aware politicians have been elected, don't sit back and wait to see what they will do. Few of Canada's politicians have technical or occupational backgrounds that prepare them for discussion and action on environmental issues. Most come from business or law, which inclines them to a certain bias. If you are concerned about particular issues, let your political representatives know about your concerns and provide them with the background information necessary to pursue action.

- ***Talk to the right people***

Many people waste a lot of energy by lobbying the wrong level of government or the wrong department. Do some homework to find out who has decision-making authority and who can influence the decision prior to taking action. Sending out a form letter won't get much attention.

Nor will asking the federal minister of the environment to intercede in an issue affecting your local landfill site, for instance. Target your lobbying for best effect.

- ***Write***

Write to politicians on issues of concern to you, even if that is all you do. Letters of praise are as important as criticisms. Politicians view letters as barometers of public opinion. Many groups try to get people to sign petitions or mail in pre-addressed postcards. These are worthwhile but they don't have the same impact as letters. Politicians know that signing a petition requires little effort, but people who sit down and write are really concerned.

If you keep your letters simple and to the point, there is a much better chance they will be read. If you write to a cabinet minister, send a copy of your letter to your own representative in government, preferably at his or her riding office. (No postage is necessary on letters addressed to politicians care of the House of Commons or your provincial legislative building.)

- ***Join***

Influencing government decisions takes considerable effort and expertise. One of the most effective ways to ensure that your concerns are recognized is to act through a group. Canada has thousands of conservation and environmental groups working on issues at all levels. Some have paid staff, but many more are run by volunteers. Each benefits from the support of a dedicated core group of supporters whose financial and volunteer assistance enables its work to continue. They all need your support.

The Canadian Environmental Movement

There are a wide range of environmental groups in Canada, each with its own focus. Some are educational and have a long-term view, others favour direct action and others are oriented toward specific projects. Politically, they cover the full spectrum, although most of the established groups have a more or less "middle-of-the-road" orientation. A list of contacts is provided in Appendix II.

At first glance, many of the major environmental organizations appear very similar. But, on closer analysis, differences in philosophy, objectives and management are readily apparent. Each group has its own priorities, which it approaches from its own perspective. The following are some of the major classes of environmental organizations, although there are few hard and fast distinctions.

- **THE EVANGELISTS**

The environmental movement has its own evangelists. Working independently, or in conjunction with one or more groups, they are eloquent and passionate speakers in defence of the environment. They play an important role in raising public awareness of issues. There is rarely an infrastructure behind these individuals, however, so don't expect more from them than some quotes, broad statistics and a lot of inspiration.

- **THE COMMANDOS**

These groups may take either a high-profile or a subversive approach to issues. Their objective is to stop things they find objectionable. Their methods include driving spikes into trees to protect them from chainsaws, or publicity stunts designed to give a high media profile to an issue. Some of these groups do more harm than good, but others play a valuable role in raising public awareness of environmental problems.

- **THE PUBLIC RESOURCE CENTRES**

These data banks and libraries monitor a wide variety of issues on behalf of the public. Their resources, and the expertise of their staffs and volunteers, make them invaluable on issues for people working at the local and provincial level.

- **THE ISSUE-ORIENTED GROUPS**

Most of the several thousand small environmental groups in Canada are organized around a single issue, either a particular environmental problem or a specific area of land. The latter may be known as "Save the ___" or "Friends of ___." Their effectiveness obviously depends on the issue and where the group is located. For example, a group in a small community attempting to protect the ozone layer can do little more than raise awareness locally. However, a group of local residents organized to protect a threatened forest in their region can have substantial impact.

- **THE WILDERNESS CRUSADERS**

Found mostly in western Canada, these groups are concerned with protecting Canada's wilderness areas for either ecological or recreational purposes. Their positions rarely differ from those of naturalists' societies, but they tend to be more focused and outspoken.

- **THE ENVIRONMENTAL GENERALISTS**

These tend to be groups with broad interests related to the environment but oriented toward pollution and human health matters. There is no clear dividing line between environmental groups and conservation groups. Their activities coincide, diverge or overlap according to the issue. Environmental networks provide a forum for smaller environmental organizations to interact at the provincial and national levels.

- **THE NATURALISTS**

Some of the oldest environmental organizations are naturalists' societies. These groups tend to represent people who participate in bird watching, botany, photography, canoeing and other outdoor pursuits that involve the appreciation of wildlife and the environment. Depending on the group, they offer social, educational and recreational activities. They have a "middle-of-the-road" orientation and an earned reputation for solid, credible work on a wide variety of issues.

- **THE LAND BUYERS**

Many groups at the provincial and national level purchase land to protect it from development, or manage land to mitigate the effects of human activities. These groups rarely become involved in public advocacy, but when they do lobby they carry a lot of weight because of their constructive approach and the fact that they bring money to the table.

- **THE HUNTERS AND ANGLERS**

Wildlife federations, fish and game associations and anglers' and hunters' groups all tend to represent people who hunt or fish for recreation. As there is no clear distinction between conservation and environmental groups, so there is no separation between wildlife federations and naturalists' societies, save for the preferred activities of members. There does tend to be a philosophical difference, but it comes to the fore only on certain issues that place the two in conflict.

The hunters and anglers represented by wildlife federations have traditionally been strong providers of volunteer and financial support for conservation.

- **THE INDUSTRIAL ORGANIZATIONS**

Most major industry associations address environmental issues from their own perspective. The petroleum industry has a separate environmental body called the Petroleum Association for the Conservation of the Environment. Some of these, such as the Canadian Chemical Producers Association (see Chapter 10), can be good sources of technical information.

- **THE PROFESSIONAL ORGANIZATIONS**

Like the industrial organizations, professional organizations bring together people such as foresters who share a similar interest. They are also a good source of technical information.

- **THE MULTIPLE-USE PROPONENTS**

There are also new groups springing up with names like "Share the ___." These are usually associated with a particular industry, and are largely made up of the industry's employees, their families and local businesspeople. These groups' purpose is to promote their side of the "preservation versus jobs" conflict. They generally argue that industrial development and protection of wilderness values can coincide in the same area.

Federal Government Programs

The federal government's environmental agency, Environment Canada, has several programs that can be helpful in your efforts to improve the environment. Every province or territory also offers a wide range of programs relating to the environment. A list of addresses to which you can write for further information is provided in Appendix III.

Environmental Choice

In 1988, the federal government announced the establishment of an "Environmentally Friendly Products" program and assembled a panel of experts to help develop criteria for selection of products. The program is designed to help you make purchasing decisions by providing a "seal of approval" to certain goods. The initiative was quickly eclipsed by the private sector when the Loblaws grocery chain came out with its "Green" line of "environmentally friendly" products.

The name of the federal program was subsequently changed to "Environmental Choice." Few products have been identified to date, as the program takes a "cradle-to-grave" approach to evaluating the environmental impact of a product and only certifies those that are as close to pure as possible. It will thus take many years before a wide range of certified products are available on the shelves. In the meantime, the opportunity to help consumers choose among a range of alternative products is ignored. Nevertheless, you can be assured that those products carrying the Environmental Choice logo, are, if not as pure as the driven snow, at least as benign as is possible.

Environmental Partners Fund

Another initiative intended to facilitate citizen action on the environment is the Environmental Partners Fund. This program, which commenced in the fall of 1989, will provide $50 million over five years to grassroots projects designed to improve the environment. Funds are awarded on a matching basis; i.e., the sponsoring organization must contribute an equivalent amount in time, resources or funds raised elsewhere.

So, if there's a river in your community that is fouled, a natural area that could be enhanced, a waste problem that could be solved by recycling or any project related to the environment that involves a "hands-on" component, support may be available through the Environmental Partners Fund. For further information, contact the nearest office of Environment Canada.

State of the Environment Reporting

In 1986, Environment Canada produced the first "State of the Environment" report. It analyzed statistics and trends relating to a variety of activities that affected the natural environment. It was a good first effort, but little data was available. The federal, provincial and territorial governments and their departments all tend to accumulate data in their own way, and standardizing the information is next to impossible.

The State of the Environment report is a valuable document nonetheless, since it represents the first step in a comprehensive effort to monitor changes to Canada's natural environment. The federal government has commenced work on the next report, to be released in 1992. Between now and then, special reports will be issued focusing on a number of sectors.

Environmental Achievement Awards
Started in 1989 by Environment Canada, the Environmental Achievement Awards recognize individuals, communities and organizations that have made a positive contribution to the Canadian environment. They are presented during Environment Week, which is celebrated the first full week in June of each year. Awards are presented in the categories of lifetime achievement, non-profit organizations, communities, corporations, media and youth.

Working With Government and Industry

Governments and many industries tend to be cumbersome and resistant to change. The booming public support for environmental protection has caught virtually everyone unprepared. While politicians and industry leaders spout environmental rhetoric, it is business as usual in most cases. Changing the system to allow it to catch up with the public's wishes is not going to be an easy task.

The environmental ethic has to become ingrained in government and business decision making at all levels if we are truly to achieve environmental protection. Due to the structure, priorities and methods of operation of government and business, it hasn't happened yet, and it isn't going to happen overnight, no matter what politicians or business leaders say. Citizens concerned about the environment must keep pointing out the inconsistencies in government policies and industry activities, either on their own or through Canada's environmental groups. We must keep the pressure on – otherwise all our individual efforts will be for naught.

16

Off We Go

OFF WE GO

Our society is at a transitional point. Modern technology has enabled us to overcome many of the obstacles to our survival. As a result, though, our ties to the natural world have been stretched to the limit and are in danger of breaking. The downside of our high levels of consumption and waste is staring us in the face.

Global climate change, acid rain, deforestation, species extinction, water pollution and resource depletion are all side effects of the benefits conferred upon us by technology. It's possible that technology alone could ensure the survival of our species, but it would be a radically different existence from the one we enjoy now. What we would lose in the process would be impossible to replace.

Alternatively, we could try to reverse growth trends, to stop technological advances, and to be content to live with less and lower our standards of living accordingly. Even if this were possible, such a drastic step may not be necessary. The challenge before us is to continue to develop as a society while remaining attuned to the natural parameters that govern our existence. To do this, first and foremost, we need to be aware of how our individual actions are contributing to the destruction of the environment. The question we all must be asking ourselves is whether we want to continue our rampage or whether we are willing to make some sacrifices to enable us to live harmoniously with our planet and other species.

Throughout this book, many practical suggestions have been made to help you start down the latter path. As important as these are, perhaps more important are the attitudes behind the actions. These are worth summarizing.

1 "Less" does not mean "worse"

Two people can live as comfortably in a 2,000-square-foot house as a 3,000-square-foot one. The smaller house may be of comparable, or higher, quality. It will require fewer natural resources to construct, furnish, heat and cool, and it might cost less. There may be no real difference in the standard of living between comparable families in both houses, just in the way their capabilities are perceived by owners and neighbours.

2 What do we really "need"?

The fact that you can afford something doesn't mean it is necessary. Owning three cars, when you can only drive one at a time, is a good example. Alternatives exist to just about everything. And many items that we are convinced we "need" end up sitting in a closet unused.

3 The "best" or most convenient product or service is not always appropriate

Nothing is environmentally friendly, but some products or practices have less severe environmental effects than others. Everything that you consume places pressure on the natural environment. By examining alternatives and modifying your purchasing decisions you can reduce your impact.

If you have always driven your car to run a certain errand, try walking, bicycling or taking the bus. Instead of using "disposable" coffee cups, use your own mug. If you frequently buy a multitude of household cleaners, consider alternatives that may be less damaging to the environment and provide similar benefits.

4 Buy the products, not the package

Many of our purchasing decisions are influenced by the way a product is packaged. We pay for the elaborate packages and then throw them in the garbage as soon as we get home, or when the product is used up. Buy the product you want with the fewest trappings possible.

5 Paying for it doesn't justify creating waste

A large portion of everything you purchase ends up in the garbage. By cutting down on waste, you reduce the quantity of natural resources being consumed in the production of these materials, and you save money.

6 **Investing time is more rewarding than saving it** Many of the products and services that contribute to our present level of environmental destruction are given to us in the name of "convenience." They save us time, which has become our most valuable commodity. Investing time, whether it is in cooking, bicycling or a family activity, can often be much more rewarding. Taking time to do something by hand can be relaxing; it can bring you in closer contact with family, friends and neighbours.

7 **Get active** Many of the alternatives to present practices require the application of calories or elbow grease. By raising your level of physical activity, you will save energy, reduce pollution and get yourself in better physical condition.

8 **Be aware** You depend on the world around you for survival, so it makes sense to learn what makes it tick. Some things that affect the environment in your community can have direct consequences to you, so it pays to become aware of what is going on before it is too late. Getting back to nature and experiencing it slowly and quietly can help you to appreciate your world and will alter your perceptions of what is important and what is not.

9 **Get off the sidelines** Taking action around the home is only one step. Extend your concern to the workplace, the community and the political level. Don't leave it up to others – ultimately, it is your quality of life that is affected by environmental degradation. Join conservation organizations and write to politicians and business leaders to pressure them to take action to protect the environment at their level.

Don't be surprised if making the changes recommended in this book improves your quality of life. Buying a smaller but equally comfortable house, replacing your car every ten years instead of every two, cycling or using public transit instead of driving, buying bulk goods instead of packaged products, changing your gardening practices and adopting different cleaning methods are all relatively simple steps that can pay off in many ways.

It is also important that we all become more informed, active and vocal on environmental issues. Unlike many of our society's problems, protecting the environment is not one that we can expect Parliament or our corporate boards to solve. It is going to take the collective effort of the public, business and governments to improve Canada's environmental performance. *We* are going to be the force that keeps the issues at the forefront. Unless individuals demonstrate through their actions that they are serious about their concern for the environment, we are not going to be able to solve the many environmental problems that beset our world. Don't leave it up to someone else.

Obviously, 26 million Canadians can have only so much influence on global problems through their individual activities. Nevertheless, Canadians *can* send a clear message to citizens of other countries. We can demonstrate that it is possible to maintain a comfortable standard of living while protecting our natural environment.

If individual Canadians can be encouraged to make even small changes in the way they live for the betterment of the environment, that is a step forward. Incremental progress is far easier to achieve than a quantum leap. Those who embrace this book's recommendations are encouraged to continue to find new ways to lessen their environmental impact. We need to critically examine every aspect of our lives from an environmental perspective, and that is a lifelong process.

Our planet is ever-changing. Global climate shifts demonstrate that. Our activities, though, are rapidly accelerating the pace of change and are coming back to haunt us. If we are to adapt as a species, then we must respond to these changes. There are no simple environmental problems and no simple solutions. But a multitude of simple responses that will lessen our impact on the environment are within the reach of every one of us. We must learn to be less wasteful and to develop an environmental ethic that includes a respect for all other species. We must recognize that we are only a part of the web of life.

APPENDIX I

Understanding Sustainable Development

"Sustainable development," the environmental catch phrase of the moment, is being used by politicians, business leaders, the media and others as a banner under which issues that affect the environment are evaluated and promoted. Unfortunately, the term is an oxymoron. The Earth's resources are not infinite, and it is therefore impossible to sustain any form of development for an indefinite period of time.

To compound matters, sustainable development means different things to different people. To exploitation advocates, it provides a rationalization for developing resources everywhere, as long as it is done in a "sustainable" fashion. To preservationists, it means putting a lid on all forms of development unless they are absolutely necessary, and sustainable beyond a shadow of a doubt. Even deciding what is to be sustained is difficult. Is it the activity itself, the economic benefits of the activity or the quality of the environment of the region in which the activity takes place?

Trying to find an acceptable definition for the term is therefore futile. However, it implies that the impacts on both the environment and the economy of a development or activity are equally important. In the past, our approach has been to move ahead for economic reasons and try, in most cases, to minimize the environmental implications. To truly ensure environmental protection, however, the impacts of a project or activity on the environment must be fully considered *before* a decision to proceed is made. Only in that way can we ensure that the project is sustainable from both an economic and an environmental perspective.

The challenge before us at the moment is to maintain the developmental orientation that has led to the standard of living enjoyed by most Canadians while reducing pressure on the natural environment. Sustainable development requires substantial changes in the way decisions are made by individuals, businesses and governments, yet it does not necessarily mean that we must all wear hair shirts and turn the clock backwards. It simply means that traditional priorities in decision making need to be modified to incorporate the impacts of all decisions on our environment.

Economic Growth

Many critics identify preoccupation with economic growth as the reason for the present environmental state of affairs. This is correct, but it does not justify the anti-growth arguments that flow from that criticism. The present view of growth relates to consumption and productivity. But economic growth does not come solely from expansion, a factor that is commonly overlooked.

We need to tackle the negative aspects of our present growth orientation. Perhaps the major problem of our present society, from an environmental perspective, is that as our affluence grows so does our waste. We are consuming more, and we are not consuming wisely. Substantial efficiencies can be achieved that will stimulate growth by reducing waste and providing new economic opportunities. By refining the way we all do business, we could experience a different type of economic growth.

How Would You Decide?

It's easy to sit back and criticize politicians for "not doing enough" to protect the environment. Politicians are judged by many criteria and, until recently, environmental protection has not been one of them. This places new pressures on the politicians and new responsibilities on the electorate. Moving toward "sustainable development" is often going to require political actions that will bring long-term benefits for the environment at the expense of short-term economic concerns. Governments traditionally look toward the next election, making "short-term pain for long-term gain" a risky proposition for them. Let's look at a hypothetical, and very simplified, example.

Imagine that you live in a small but booming town that revolves around a sawmill. The town is represented in government by the ruling party. Due to forestry activity in the entire region, the timber supply is under great pressure. In order to ensure the sustainability of the resource, the government makes a decision to restrict timber quotas to reduce the pressure. This will mean that your town and its industry will remain viable for many more years than would otherwise have been possible.

However, less wood is available for your sawmill, and the short-term consequence is that the local mill reduces its workforce. This has a ripple effect on the entire economy. You lose your job, or your business declines. Several family members and friends share a similar fate, and some move away. Your house becomes devalued, or even impossible to sell. The social, recreational, cultural and economic activity of the town slows.

During the next election, do you vote for your present representative because of his government's long-term concern for the environment, or do you throw him out for the economic consequences that have followed? If you were represented by a member of the opposition, who campaigned against the decision, would you vote her back in for supporting your town's economy or vote her out for opposing environmental protection?

Until politicians are convinced that environmental protection will win them support at the polls, they are going to be very reluctant to make the tough decisions. Are we going to support them?

Obstacles To Sustainable Development

Many governments and industries are using the term "sustainable development" to rationalize existing projects or policies when it is rarely appropriate. In addressing environmental issues, there are a number of obstacles, symbolic of the lack of consensus on the meaning of sustainable development, that frequently rear their heads. When following issues in the media, or working on them yourself, you may encounter some of the following common arguments.

▪ ***We need the jobs and economic benefits/We must remain competitive***

This argument attests to the prevalence of economic concerns in decision making. It usually involves the subsidization of high-risk activities that may otherwise be unfeasible. It is the reason why, in Canada, it is often cheaper to extract natural resources, such as lumber, minerals and oil, than to promote conservation or recycling. It also encourages wasteful and environmentally damaging agricultural practices. It is *the* major obstacle to be overcome if environmental protection and economic development are to be reconciled.

▪ ***Prove that this project, chemical, etc., will damage the environment!***

In determining whether a project, procedure or chemical is approved, the burden of proof is always placed on the opponents, while the proponent is considered innocent until proven guilty. The right way to grant someone permission to do something that may affect the health of the environment and the people that live within it would be to ensure, as far as possible, that it is safe before making the decision to proceed. That does not yet happen in Canada. It generally takes far longer to secure approval to market a new drug than to get approval to proceed with a pulp mill, for example.

▪ ***We'll cross the environmental bridge when we come to it***

As mentioned above, many governments and regulatory agencies tend to approve projects first and ask environmental questions later. Consequently, arguments almost always focus on how to mitigate the ill effects of the project rather than on whether the project makes environmental sense in the first place. Once approval is granted, momentum builds and money starts to be spent, reducing the chances of stopping the project. Many interpret sustainable development to mean increased attention to mitigation.

▪ ***Environmental protection costs a lot***

Protecting the environment appears expensive because, until recently, it has never been considered a true cost of doing business. The downside of economic development was either ignored or addressed through governments, and the cost was hidden in our taxes. Now, protecting the environment is supposedly a fact of life. In the short term, that will mean that prices for a lot of goods are going to increase as costs are passed along to the consumer. In that respect, environmental protection is no different from any other business consideration.

▪ ***Sustainable development doesn't apply to me***

Many self-proclaimed conservationists

will line up behind a project in their area that they would lobby against anywhere else if it might bring them advantage. For many people, environmental protection is an absolute priority unless it's their ox that is being gored. Think globally, act locally – even if it hurts.

▪ ***Jobs versus trees, owls, butterflies, etc.***

The simplified "environment versus economy" conflict will never go away, no matter how hard we try to reconcile the two. The problem is obviously more acute at the local level, where individuals can directly benefit or lose from an environmental decision. However, it is also a concern on a broader scale. An industry might argue that installing pollution control equipment will result in lay-offs, for example. The challenge is to find ways to retain jobs *and* protect the environment, but that goal is easy to lose in the rhetoric and emotion that ensues.

▪ ***We have the technology!***

No, we don't. Ecosystems are incredibly complex, and anyone, no matter what their academic qualifications, who claims to be able to accurately predict the impact of a project, positively or negatively, should be looked upon with skepticism. We don't know much about how nature works. All we can do is gather as much information as possible, evaluate the probabilities, and learn from our past experiences – something we aren't very good at.

Implementing Sustainable Development

Since sustainable development is open to a wide range of interpretations, nobody can claim to have the "right" answer. Nor, in many situations, is there a right answer. What is important is that we recognize that economic activity can no longer be conducted in a short-sighted manner. Environmental protection must be just as important as economic development if we, and our children, are to survive on this planet. The first step in reconciling the two is to broaden the participation in the decision-making process.

Most jurisdictions have set up "round tables" on the environment and the economy. These are intended to bring representatives of government, industry, environmental groups, academia and the public together to discuss the way in which we do business, and look for ways in which we can satisfy both environmental and economic objectives. This is an important process. But unless action is quickly taken "on the ground," where it counts, this exercise will be ineffective.

The principles of sustainable development don't apply only to major economic activities. They can also be applied every day within our own homes, workplaces and communities. We all need to think of the environment in all of our decisions. If we can't do that, and make the relatively small sacrifices necessary, we can hardly expect success on a global scale. Ultimately, responsibility rests with all of us. How you define sustainable development doesn't matter. What you do does.

APPENDIX II

Plugging In to the Environmental Movement

No one can combat alone the multitude of environmental issues the world faces today. But take heart – no matter what issue concerns you, someone, somewhere, is battling a similar problem. There is strength in numbers, and you can acquire that strength by joining an established environmental group or networking with a number of smaller groups and individuals who are addressing similar issues elsewhere.

Joining a local environmental group will provide you with a multitude of benefits. You will meet people who, like you, are concerned about the environment and are acting on their concerns. These contacts can provide you with moral support and a wealth of information. Your knowledge of issues and ways of approaching them will increase considerably.

Adding your voice and talents to these groups' existing campaigns is far more efficient than trying to re-invent the wheel by yourself. They need your support. None of Canada's environmental groups are wealthy, and the vast majority lead a hand-to-mouth existence that belies the importance of their work. Similar groups at each of the local, provincial and national levels address different issues or the same ones, in a different way. If you truly want to become involved, support groups at all levels.

CONTRIBUTING FINANCIALLY

A lot of groups are asking for money these days to fight environmental battles. Most fund-raising material is pretty generic and doesn't provide much information on the real work of the organization. Deciding where to funnel your financial support, however modest, is not a simple task. The following points will help in evaluating organizations.

1. Ask for an audited financial statement and an annual report. (Note: Smaller groups don't prepare annual reports.) Don't give money to any group that will not provide you with a financial statement.
2. Examine the organization's history and track record. How long has it been in existence? What issues has it fought? What credibility has it earned with decision makers? If it is a newly formed group, does it duplicate the work of existing organizations and, if so, why?
3. Find out who calls the shots. Who is on the board of directors? How are the directors selected and to whom are they accountable? As a contributor, do you have a vote in the organization's affairs?

4. What proportion of the organization's budget is devoted to fund raising? Fund raising is an expensive but necessary business for all charitable organizations. The good ones keep fund-raising costs to a minimum. If fund-raising costs exceed 20% of receipts from membership fees and donations, there had better be a good explanation.

5. Compare the amount of donations received to the amount expended on the organization's charitable activities and programs. If the former is more than the latter, then you aren't getting value for the dollar; the wider the gap, the more of your money the organization is wasting.

6. Evaluate what you get for your money. If you are joining as a member, what services is the organization providing for the membership fee, and are they worth the price?

National Environmental Groups

Canadian Arctic Resources Committee
111 Sparks Street, 4th Floor
Ottawa, Ontario, K1P 5B5
613-236-7379
A small but highly credible and respected group working on northern issues, including environmental concerns.

Canadian Federation of Humane Societies
30 Concourse Gate, Suite 102
Nepean, Ontario, K2E 7V7
613-224-8072
The national association of Canadian animal welfare organizations is primarily concerned with the welfare of pets, livestock and laboratory animals.

Canadian Forestry Association
185 Somerset Street West, Suite 203
Ottawa, Ontario, K2P 0J2
613-232-1815
This national federation of provincial forestry associations seeks to promote awareness, understanding and sustainable development of Canada's forests. In order to maintain its objectivity, it does not take any money from the forestry industry.

Canadian Nature Federation
453 Sussex Drive
Ottawa, Ontario, K1N 6Z4
613-238-6154
800-267-4088
Canada's national naturalists' organization has an extensive array of advocacy and educational programs. It publishes *Nature Canada* magazine (founded in 1939) and operates the Nature Canada Bookshop, Canada's largest mail-order selection of books, optical equipment, clothing and other products to help you enhance your appreciation of nature.

Canadian Parks and Wilderness Society
160 Bloor Street East, Suite 1150
Toronto, Ontario, M4W 1B9
416-972-0868
A nation-wide group devoted exclusively to parks and wilderness issues. Organized in chapters around the country. It publishes the quarterly magazine *Borealis*.

Canadian Wildlife Federation
1673 Carling Avenue
Ottawa, Ontario, K2A 3Z1
613-725-2191
The national organization of anglers and hunters, CWF is also supported by non-voting associate members. It publishes the magazines *International Wildlife*, *Ranger Rick* and *Your Big Backyard* and distributes them to members. CWF also operates a sizeable mail-order merchandising business.

Ducks Unlimited
1190 Waverley Street
Winnipeg, Manitoba, R3T 2E2
204-477-1760
This international organization exists to preserve and restore habitat for waterfowl and other wetland creatures. Its funding comes primarily from hunters, and a large part of its Canadian budget is contributed by its American partner. No other group, private or government, is doing more to protect wetlands.

Energy Probe
225 Brunswick Avenue
Toronto, Ontario, M5S 2M6
416-978-7014
An offshoot of Pollution Probe, this group, as its name implies, is devoted to energy matters. It is one of the leading critics of the nuclear industry in Canada.

Friends of the Earth
251 Laurier Avenue West, Suite 701
Ottawa, Ontario, K1P 5J6
613-230-3352
The Canadian arm of this international environmental group is a small but rapidly growing organization. The acronym, FOE, conveniently represents its chosen role as a watchdog of industry and government. Few are better at pointing out the hypocrisies of government.

Greenpeace
578 Bloor Street West
Toronto, Ontario, M6G 1K1
416-538-6470
Born in Canada, this huge international organization is the "people's front" for the environment. It employs confrontation and aggressive media tactics to draw attention to environmental problems. Nobody points fingers better than Greenpeace.

Indigenous Survival International
47 Clarence Street
Ottawa, Ontario, K1N 9K1
613-236-0673
This organization approaches environmental issues from the perspective of native peoples. It has been particularly vocal against threats to the fur industry.

Nature Conservancy of Canada
794A Broadview Avenue
Toronto, Ontario, M4K 2P7
416-469-1701
Its U.S counterpart is one of that country's most effective conservation organizations and has acquired an impressive land bank. When an area is threatened by development, they don't protest, they buy it! The Canadian organization is much smaller but is well on its way to establishing a similar network of reserves and sanctuaries.

Pollution Probe
12 Madison Avenue
Toronto, Ontario, M5R 2S1
416-926-1907
One of the most constructive environmental groups. While Pollution Probe takes on a watchdog role and delights in pointing fingers, it also promotes resolutions to problems that are in the best interests of all parties. It has the ear of industry and government.

Probe International
225 Brunswick Avenue
Toronto, Ontario, M5S 2M6
416-978-7014
An offshoot of Energy Probe, Probe International focuses its attention on environmental issues in the developing world, with a particular interest in the policies of lending institutions and aid organizations.

Rawson Academy of Aquatic Science
1 Nicholas Street, Suite 404
Ottawa, Ontario, K1N 7B7
613-563-2636
A highly respected and credible group focusing on fish and the aquatic environment. Although small, it is involved in a wide range of issues.

Wildlife Habitat Canada
1704 Carling Avenue, Suite 301
Ottawa, Ontario, K2A 1C7
613-722-2090
Formed in 1984, WHC was created by a coalition of non-governmental organizations and governments that saw a definite need for a group that would focus exclusively on habitat preservation. One revenue source is the sale of an annual "duck stamp" with hunting licences. It is active on a wide range of habitat issues all across Canada.

World Wildlife Fund (Canada)
60 St. Clair Avenue East, Suite 201
Toronto, Ontario, M4T 1N5
416-923-8173
If you want your dollars to go directly to conservation projects "on the ground," the Canadian arm of this international organization gives you the best value for the dollar. WWF funds hundreds of research, educational and action projects across the country each year.

World Society for the Protection of Animals
215 Lakeshore Boulevard East
Suite 211
Toronto, Ontario, M5A 3W9
416-369-0044
This international animal welfare organization is the only such group recognized by the United Nations. It operates a wide range of programs worldwide, including disaster relief and provision of veterinary aid in developing countries.

TWO AMERICAN GROUPS
Environmental issues respect no borders, and there is frequent interaction between Canadian and American organizations. Two prominent U.S. groups are:

Defenders of Wildlife
1244 19th Street N.W.
Washington, D.C., 20036
U.S.A.
202-659-9510
Defenders is an active advocate for wildlife and wildlife habitat. It publishes the bi-monthly magazine *Defenders*. One of its major campaigns focuses on the problems caused by marine debris.

National Audubon Society
950 Third Avenue
New York, New York, 10022
U.S.A.
212-832-3200
The American equivalent of the Canadian Nature Federation. NAS is active on a number of "transboundary" issues, including acid rain and hydroelectric exports. Publishes *Audubon* magazine.

Provincial Naturalist Groups

These groups are very active on the conservation scene at the provincial level. They not only work on issues but also provide social, educational and recreational experiences for their members that can greatly increase understanding and appreciation of the natural world. In the larger provinces, they can also refer you to more local clubs in your area.

Newfoundland Natural History Society
P.O. Box 1013
St. John's, Newfoundland, A1C 5M3

Nova Scotia Bird Society
c/o The Nova Scotia Museum
1747 Summer Street
Halifax, Nova Scotia, B3H 3A6

New Brunswick Federation of Naturalists
277 Douglas Avenue
Saint John, New Brunswick, E2K 1E5

Natural History Society of Prince Edward Island
53 Fitzroy Street
Charlottetown, Prince Edward Island
C1A 1R4

Union québécoise pour la conservation de la nature
160 – 76 Street E., 2nd floor
Charlesbourg, Quebec, G1H 4R3

Province of Quebec Society for the Protection of Birds
240 – 36th Avenue
Lachine, Quebec, H8T 2A3

Federation of Ontario Naturalists
355 Lesmill Road
Don Mills, Ontario, M3B 2W8

Manitoba Naturalists Society
302 – 128 James Avenue
Winnipeg, Manitoba, R3B 0N8

Saskatchewan Natural History Society
P.O. Box 4348
Regina, Saskatchewan, S4P 3W6

Federation of Alberta Naturalists
P.O. Box 1472
Edmonton, Alberta, T5J 2N5

Ecology North
P.O. Box 2888
Yellowknife, Northwest Territories
X1A 2N1

Yukon Conservation Society
P.O. Box 4163
Whitehorse, Yukon, Y1A 3S9

Federation of British Columbia Naturalists
321 – 1367 West Broadway
Vancouver, British Columbia, V6H 4A9

Other Environmental Organizations

Several other environmental organizations have been referred to in the text of this book in relation to specific issues. Here's where you can contact them for further information.

Alberta Wilderness Association
455 – 12th Street N.W.
Calgary, Alberta, T2N 1Y9

Environmentally Sound Packaging Coalition
2150 Maple Street
Vancouver, British Columbia, V6J 3T3

Friends of Ecological Reserves
P.O. Box 1721, Station E
Victoria, British Columbia, V8W 2Y1

Friends of the Athabasca Environmental Association
Box 1351
Athabasca, Alberta, T0G 0B0

Société pour vaincre la pollution
C.P. 65, Succursale Place d'Armes
Montreal, Quebec, H2Y 3E9

Temagami Wilderness Society
19 Mercer Street, Suite 307
Toronto, Ontario, M5V 1H2

Western Canada Wilderness Committee
20 Water Street
Vancouver, British Columbia, V6B 1A4

Environmental Networks

Interested in a specific issue and want to know who's working on it in your region? Then contact your regional environment network. Established to allow smaller groups concentrating on their own issues to come together and share information and expertise, the networks facilitate the exchange of information among groups and are an excellent way to contact groups working in your area or on issues of concern to you around the country.

Canadian Environmental Network
P.O. Box 1289, Station B
Ottawa, Ontario, K1P 5R3
613-563-2078

Atlantic Environmental Network
3115 Veith Street, 3rd Floor
Halifax, Nova Scotia, B3K 3G9
902-454-2139

Réseau québécois des groupes écologistes
C.P. 1480, Succursale Place d'Armes
Montreal, Quebec, H2Y 3K8
514-982-9444

Ontario Environment Network
456 Spadina Avenue, 2nd Floor
Toronto, Ontario, M5T 2G8
416-925-1322

Manitoba Eco-Network
P.O. Box 3125
Winnipeg, Manitoba, R3C 4E6
204-956-1468

Saskatchewan Eco-Network
P.O. Box 1372
Saskatoon, Saskatchewan, S7K 0G4
306-665-1915

Alberta Environmental Network
10511 Saskatchewan Drive
Edmonton, Alberta, T6E 4S1
403-465-0872

Northern Environmental Network
P.O. Box 4163
Whitehorse, Yukon, Y1A 3S9
403-668-5687

British Columbia Environmental Network
2150 Maple Street
Vancouver, British Columbia, V6J 3T3
604-733-2400

APPENDIX III

Government Contacts

The federal, provincial and territorial governments all have programs in place on a wide variety of environmental matters. They produce a phenomenal amount of literature and often have more intensive programs to promote citizen involvement or action. If you live in a large city, your local government may offer similar services.

THE FEDERAL GOVERNMENT

Environment Canada
Communications Directorate
Hull, Quebec, K1A 0H3
613-997-6820

REGIONAL OFFICES
Environment Canada
Atlantic Region
15th Floor, 45 Alderney Drive
Dartmouth, Nova Scotia, B2Y 2N6
902-426-1930

Environment Canada
Quebec Region
C.P. 6060, Succursale Haute-Ville
Quebec, Quebec, G1R 4V7
418-648-7204

Environment Canada
Ontario Region
25 St. Clair Avenue East, 6th Floor
Toronto, Ontario, M4T 1M2
416-973-1093

Environment Canada
Western and Northern Region
2nd Floor, 4999 – 98 Avenue
Edmonton, Alberta, T6B 2X3
403-468-8074

Environment Canada
Pacific and Yukon Region
Communications Directorate
3rd Floor, Kapilano 100
Park Royal South
West Vancouver, British Columbia
V7T 1A2
604-666-5902

PROVINCIAL AND TERRITORIAL GOVERNMENTS

NEWFOUNDLAND
Department of Environment and Lands
P.O. Box 8700
St. John's, Newfoundland, A1B 4J6
709-576-3394

Department of Forestry and Agriculture
P.O. Box 8700
St. John's, Newfoundland, A1B 4J6
709-576-3760

NOVA SCOTIA
Department of the Environment
P.O. Box 2107
Halifax, Nova Scotia, B3J 3B7
902-424-5300

Department of Lands and Forests
P.O. Box 698
Halifax, Nova Scotia, B3J 2T9
902-424-6694

NEW BRUNSWICK
Department of the Environment
P.O. Box 6000
Fredericton, New Brunswick, E3B 5H1
506-453-3700

Department of Natural Resources and Energy
P.O. Box 6000
Fredericton, New Brunswick, E3B 5H1
506-453-2614

PRINCE EDWARD ISLAND
Department of the Environment
P.O. Box 2000
Charlottetown, Prince Edward Island C1A 7N8
902-368-5000

Department of Energy and Forestry
P.O. Box 2000
Charlottetown, Prince Edward Island C1A 7N8
902-368-5010

QUEBEC
Ministère de l'Environnement
3900, rue Marly
Ste-Foy, Quebec, G1X 4E4
418-643-6071

Ministère du Loisir, de la Chasse et de la Pêche
150, boul. St-Cyrille Est
Quebec, Quebec, G1K 4Y1
418-643-2984

ONTARIO
Ministry of the Environment
135 St. Clair Avenue West
Toronto, Ontario, M4V 1P5
416-323-4324

Ministry of Natural Resources
Whitney Block, 99 Wellesley Street West
Toronto, Ontario, M7A 1W3
416-965-3315

MANITOBA
Manitoba Environment
330 St. Mary Avenue
Winnipeg, Manitoba, R3C 3Z5
204-945-5763

Manitoba Natural Resources
1495 St. James Street
Winnipeg, Manitoba, R3H 0W9
204-945-6784

SASKATCHEWAN
Saskatchewan Environment and Public Safety
3085 Albert Street
Regina, Saskatchewan, S4S 0B1
306-787-6113

Saskatchewan Parks and Renewable Resources
3211 Albert Street
Regina, Saskatchewan, S4S 5W6
306-787-2322

ALBERTA
Alberta Environment
Oxbridge Place
9820 – 106 Street
Edmonton, Alberta, T5K 2J6
403-427-2739

Alberta Forestry, Lands and Wildlife
9920 – 108 Street
Edmonton, Alberta, T5K 2M4
403-427-3590

BRITISH COLUMBIA
Ministry of Environment
Public Affairs and Communications Branch
810 Blanshard Street
Victoria, British Columbia, V8V 1X5
604-387-9419

Ministry of Parks
4000 Seymour Place, 3rd Floor
Victoria, British Columbia, V8V 1X4
604-387-5002

Ministry of Forests
595 Pandora Avenue
Victoria, British Columbia, V8W 3E7
604-387-5255

NORTHWEST TERRITORIES
Department of Renewable Resources
P.O. Box 2668
Yellowknife, Northwest Territories X1A 2P9
403-873-7181

YUKON TERRITORY
Department of Renewable Resources
P.O. Box 2703
Whitehorse, Yukon, Y1A 2C6
403-667-5721

BIBLIOGRAPHY

The following are some suggested titles to provide you with more in-depth information relating to the topics covered in this book. Most of these can be obtained through the Nature Canada Bookshop, 453 Sussex Drive, Ottawa, Ontario, K1N 6Z4, 800-267-4088. The Nature Canada Bookshop stocks several hundred books relating to nature and the outdoors, as well as optical equipment, clothing and gift items. All proceeds from sales support the conservation work of the Canadian Nature Federation.

Barash, David P. *The Hare and the Tortoise: Culture, Biology and Human Nature.* New York: Viking Penguin, 1986.

Bird, Peter M., and David J. Rapport. *State of the Environment Report for Canada.* Ottawa: Supply and Services Canada, 1986.

Burnett, J. A., C. T. Dauphiné, S. H. McCrindle and T. Mosquin. *On the Brink: Endangered Species in Canada.* Saskatoon: Western Producer Prairie Books, 1989.

Cousteau, Jacques-Yves. *The Cousteau Almanac.* New York: Doubleday, 1981.

Day, David. *The Eco Wars: True Tales of Environmental Madness.* Toronto: Key Porter Books, 1989.

Dennis, John V. *A Complete Guide to Bird Feeding.* New York: Knopf, 1975.

Drushka, Ken. *Stumped: The Forestry Industry in Transition.* Vancouver: Douglas & McIntyre, 1985.

Ernest, Ruth Shaw. *The Naturalist's Garden: Bring Your Yard to Life with Plants and Attract Wildlife.* Emmaus, PA: Rodale Press, 1987.

Evernden, Neil. *The Natural Alien: Humankind and Environment.* Toronto: University of Toronto Press, 1985.

Friday, Laurie, and Ronald Laskey, eds. *The Fragile Environment: The Darwin College Lectures.* Cambridge: Cambridge University Press, 1989.

Giono, Jean. *The Man Who Planted Trees.* Chelsea, VT: Chelsea Green Publishers, 1985.

Hampton, Bruce, and David Cole. *Soft Paths: How to Enjoy the Wilderness Without Harming It.* Harrisburg: Stackpole Books, 1988.

Hummel, Monte. *Endangered Spaces: The Future for Canada's Wilderness.* Toronto: Key Porter Books, 1989.

Keating, Michael. *To the Last Drop: Canada and the World's Water Crisis.* Toronto: Macmillan, 1986.

Leopold, Aldo. *A Sand County Almanac: And Sketches Here and There.* New York: Oxford University Press, 1949.

Lovelock, James. *The Ages of Gaia: A Biography of Our Living Earth.* New York: Norton, 1988.

MacEwan, Grant. *Entrusted to My Care.* Saskatoon: Western Producer Prairie Books, 1986.

Merilees, Bill. *Attracting Backyard Wildlife: A Guide for Nature-Lovers.* Vancouver: Whitecap Books, 1989.

Riotte, Louise. *Carrots Love Tomatoes: Secrets of Companion Planting for Successful Gardening.* Pownal, VT: Storey Communications, 1975.

Riotte, Louise. *Roses Love Garlic: Secrets of Companion Planting with Flowers.* Pownal, VT: Storey Communications, 1983.

Seymour, John, and Herbert Girardet. *Blueprint for a Green Planet.* New York: Prentice-Hall, 1987.

Swift, Jamie. *Cut and Run: The Assault on Canada's Forests.* Toronto: Between the Lines, 1983.

Waterman, Laura, and Guy Waterman. *Backwoods Ethics: Environmental Concerns for Hikers and Campers.* Washington, D.C.: Stone Wall Press, 1979.

INDEX

Z